rd W. Krakeur - Rober

presc

Arthur Kennedy -

in

E LOUD RED PATRICK

A NEW COMEDY
by John Boruff

Suggested by the novel of
the same name by Ruth McKenney

Directed by Robert Douglas

Scenery, Costumes and Lighting
by Paul Morrison

SAMUEL FRENCH, INC.

25 WEST 45TH STREET   NEW YORK 36

7624 SUNSET BOULEVARD   HOLLYWOOD 46

LONDON   *TORONTO*

THE LOUD RED PATRICK

THE CAST

As Played at the Opening
October 3, 1956
at The Ambassador Theatre, New York City

(In order of appearance)

10 ROSALIE FLANNIGAN .... *Kimetha Laurie*
7 RITA FLANNIGAN .... *Renne Jarrett*
17 MAGGIE FLANNIGAN .... *Peggy Maurer*
16 MARY FLANNIGAN .... *Nancy Devlin*
middle age MRS. GALLUP .... *Mary Farrell*
mid 40's PATRICK FLANNIGAN .... *Arthur Kennedy*
MR. FINNEGAN .... *David Wayne*
RALPH PENROSE .... *James Congdon*
RICHARD .... *James Karr*

SYNOPSIS OF SCENES

*The entire action of the play takes place in the Flannigan
living-room, in Cleveland, Ohio, mid-August, 1912.*

ACT ONE
Late afternoon—Tuesday.

ACT TWO
Thursday afternoon.

ACT THREE
The following day—early morning.

4

The Loud Red Patrick

ACT ONE

SET DESCRIPTION: *Living room of the Flannigan home, period 1912. The decor, though cheerful, reflects the ugliness of the period. Down Right a bay window with open drapes. Up Right front door with glass paneling which permits a glimpse of shrubs and vines outside. Both the entrance to the house and the stairs to the second floor give onto a platform or landing one step above the living room level. Up Center stairs, stained glass window half way up. Up Left Center an alcove with sliding drapes. Door Left leading to kitchen. Down Right secretary and chair. Waste basket above secretary. Up Right on landing a 1912 Victrola. Down Right Center a Morris chair and footstool. Center an oval table. Left Center an arm chair. Down Center andirons to suggest a fireplace. Up Center built-in bench with cushions. Down Left chaise lounge with cushions. Up Right Center an old-fashioned crank telephone is hung on the wall. Up Center an occasional chair. Up Left directly adjacent to alcove is a sideboard with wine, liquors and glassware. Up Left a chair. Down Left an occasional chair.*

AT RISE: *The stage is empty. Outside comes the sound of a 1912 AUTOMOBILE arriving with honks and racket. Cries of "Goodbye" "Thank you" and general excitement. MRS. GALLUP comes from kitchen entrance. She is a fluttery, spinsterish widow of middle age. Taking off her apron, she rushes across to window seat and looks out. RITA, age 7, ROSALIE, age 10, and MARY, age 16, run in front door.*

5

ROSALIE. Oh, what wonderful fun! What a beautiful autocar!

MRS. GALLUP. Shhhh! Shhhh! Children! Children! I just cleaned this living room. *(To* ROSALIE *and* RITA*)* Into the yard with you. Go on—

ROSALIE. *(Exiting Left)* Let's play Stanley Steamer in the old carriage!

RITA. First one to the carriage house gets to be driver.

(They run off Left.)

MARY. *(Glancing out window)* Oh, look! He's kissing her hand! Mrs. Gallup! Guess what! *(Turns to her)* Maggie's secretly engaged!

MRS. GALLUP. *(Startled)* What! Why, my land! *(To Right of chaise.)*

MARY. He came here this afternoon and took us all for a ride in his Stanley Steamer and—he proposed to her in Cincinnati.

MAGGIE. *(Entering front door—to Left of* MARY. *She is an attractive girl of 17)* Oh Mary! After you swore!

MRS. GALLUP. *(Crosses Center, worried)* Maggie—who is this young man? Don't tell me you've gotten engaged to some perfect stranger?

MAGGIE. *(Crosses to her)* His name is Ralph Penrose.

MRS. GALLUP. Penrose? The Penrose Gas Company! Imagine what your father will say when he hears it's the gas company!

MARY. *(Eagerly)* How did he propose, Maggie? Was he romantic?

MAGGIE. *(Sits Right arm of Morris chair. Dreamily)* Oh, yes, he certainly was! He did it on one knee with his straw hat over his heart.

MRS. GALLUP. *(Crosses; sits Left Center)* Oh, I don't like the look of it, Maggie, getting engaged before the families have met.

MAGGIE. *(Crosses up Center, with suppressed excitement)* That's not the worst of it, Mrs. Gallup. Ralph doesn't just want to be engaged—he wants to get married.

MARY. *(Right of Morris chair)* Well—of course. Isn't that what an engagement means?

MAGGIE. Silly. The point is—he wants to get married *now!*

MARY. *(Mouth open. Deliciously shocked)* Now—?

MRS. GALLUP. My goodness! That's just not possible! Your father would never permit it.

MAGGIE. *(A little crestfallen)* Papa's going to be a problem I know.

MARY. Gosh, yes. You're supposed to start college in the fall.

MAGGIE. *(Left of Morris chair)* Vassar hasn't accepted me yet—

MARY. Papa will send you somewhere. You know Papa and education.

MRS. GALLUP. *(Thinks)* And this college business is such nonsense, too. You know the kind of women that go to such places. Never catch me there I can tell you. *(Sighs)* But—if that's the way your father wants it—

MAGGIE. *(Determined)* What I want is going to have to count for something from now on.

MRS. GALLUP. I'm afraid it's not in the cards for you, dear— *(She is struck with a thought)* The cards—I wonder—I just wonder—

MARY. *(Crossing to Right of her)* Have you got an idea, Mrs. Gallup?

MRS. GALLUP. Could it be— *(Takes out piece of paper, glances at it thoughtfully)* Oh, no, it must be meant for me—

MAGGIE. What?

MRS. GALLUP. Well, I—I visited my fortune teller this afternoon—Madame Jeremiah—and she gave me a very strange prediction. I hoped it was for me, but could it be— Listen to this— *(Reads.)*

> "When and where you least expect it
> Comes a man who's strong and brave
> To carry you and all your burdens
> Forever after—till the grave."

MARY. Gee—that's real spooky, isn't it! And it could be for Maggie.

MAGGIE. Heavens!

MRS. GALLUP. No—no, I don't think it is for Maggie either. Madame Jeremiah distinctly asked the spirit about my future.

(PATRICK FLANNIGAN *enters front door. He is a big, hearty, open Irishman in his middle forties. He has only the trace of an Irish lilt in his speech.*)

PATRICK. *(Big booming voice)* I'm home, everybody! *(He crosses down Right Center.)*

(MAGGIE *and* MARY *cross to him.*)

MRS. GALUP. You always take me by surprise with that bellow of yours!

PATRICK. Did I bellow, Mrs. Gallup? I'm sorry. And how are my darlings?

MAGGIE. *(Right of him)* Hello, Papa—

MARY. *(Left of him)* Fine, Papa—

(PATRICK *fishes in briefcase, takes out a book, comes over to* MAGGIE, *who stands rather stiffly. She is tensed with nervousness.* PATRICK *puts one finger under her chin and lifts her face.*)

PATRICK. Any news today—? *(Studies her face a moment, drops finger.)*

    (MARY *sits chaise.*)

No, it still didn't come, did it?

MAGGIE. What, Papa—?

PATRICK. The letter from Vassar.

    (MAGGIE *shakes head, glancing at* MARY. MARY *crosses Right.*)

I know. I have only to look at your face and I can tell.

Well, cheer up. It will be here any day now. Where's the rest of the brood?

MARY. Outside, I think.

PATRICK. *(Holds out book to* MAGGIE*)* There!

MAGGIE. What's this, Papa?

PATRICK. *(Sits Morris chair)* Look at it. That should be of special interest to you, I think.

MAGGIE. *(Reading title)* "Woman's Rights and the Law"—well—thank you, Papa. *(She kisses him.)*

PATRICK. After you finish your college, you should go on and study the law, Maggie. You've got a fine mind for it, child.

MRS. GALLUP. Women lawyers! What next!

PATRICK. Women doctors, women merchants, women chiefs and women voters, Mrs. Gallup, that's what's next. We stand at the threshold of a new era of progress when the female will become something more than a mere breeder of the species.

MRS. GALLUP. *(Rises)* Mr. Flannigan! Please refrain from such expressions in my presence.

PATRICK. You have a deep contempt for your sex, mam, but I do not share it.

(MRS. GALLUP *sweeps towards kitchen door.)*
And forgive me if I use the word sex!

(She gives a little start as he repeats the word. MRS. GALLUP *exits.* PATRICK *smiles.)*

MAGGIE. Papa, you shouldn't.

PATRICK. Nonsense. I'm allowed to shock her once a day. We all agreed on that.

(MAGGIE *crosses; sits Left of table.)*
What's the matter? Don't you like the book? *(Rises; crosses down stage.)*

MAGGIE. Yes, Papa—it's very nice. I—hope I'm up to it.

PATRICK. *(At fireplace)* Nonsense. Of course you're up to it.

MRS. GALLUP. *(Bursts back in from kitchen)* Mr. Flannigan! I demand to know who put garter snakes in my preserve jars.

PATRICK. Well, don't look at me, Mrs. Gallup. I'm too old for such things. *(Sitting Morris chair.)*

MRS. GALLUP. *(Above table)* And I'm too old to work in a kitchen that's crawling with wild beasts! Mr. Flannigan, I demand that you speak to Rita and Rosalie about this! They're planning a whole collection!

PATRICK. I consider that highly educational, ma'am.

MRS. GALLUP. I consider it disgusting! I've tried to change their minds but—

PATRICK. Mrs. Gallup, you have one standing order here—you change their diapers—*I'll* change their minds!

MRS. GALLUP. *(Crossing Left)* Indeed. Well, that leaves me with little to do then, since by some miracle they *are* at least house-broken. *(Nose in air, she exits into kitchen.)*

PATRICK. *(Looking after, chuckles)* Ah, that woman! Study her carefully, girls. She is the perfect example of what you must all grow up *not* to be.

MAGGIE. *(Indicating for MARY to go. She does, up stairs)* Papa—could I talk to you a minute?

PATRICK. Of course.

MAGGIE. *(Crosses above table)* —There's a young man I'd like to invite to dinner Thursday. He's very anxious to meet you— *(Lighting his pipe.)*

PATRICK. Oh? Who's that?

MAGGIE. Someone I met at Aunt Ruth's in Cincinnati. His name is—well—it's Ralph Penrose—

PATRICK. Penrose? Penrose! Not the Gas Company's son! Maggie Flannigan, you know my opinion of the Penrose family!

MAGGIE. You don't even know them!

PATRICK. Oh, don't I!

MAGGIE. Not personally, no.

PATRICK. Must I know the devil personally to know he's the devil. For ten years I've been fighting the evils perpetrated on this city by that Penrose tribe!

MAGGIE. *(Kneels Left of him)* But Ralph's not like the rest of his family.

PATRICK. He's a branch of the main gas main, is he not?

MAGGIE. He's not a branch of anything. He's a person in his own right as you'll see when you meet him.

PATRICK. *(Rises, crosses down Right)* I'll not meet him. You well know it's not my habit to consort with my enemies!

MAGGIE. *(Rises)* Enemies!

PATRICK. *(Crosses up Right Center)* Yes! Are they not fighting tooth and nail to block the coming of electric lights? Downtown Cleveland is ablaze with the glory of Mr. Edison's work, but out here we stumble in the darkness of gas light. They stand four square in the path of progress! And I say they're a disgrace to the community! *(Sits chair Right.)*

MAGGIE. I know, Papa, I've read all your letters to the papers. But you might at least *meet* Ralph and talk to him. *(As PATRICK still hesitates)* Are you afraid to meet him?

PATRICK. Afraid! I'll show you who's afraid. *(Considering a moment)* I'll talk with the boy!

MAGGIE. *(Crosses and gets book)* I think you'll be surprised. I think you'll like him.

PATRICK. All right. Let him come. We'll see about that.

MAGGIE. *(Kisses him)* Oh, thank you, Papa. (MAGGIE *exits upstairs.)*

(FINNEGAN's *RING and special TAP is heard.)*

PATRICK. *(Rises)* Good, there's Finnegan. Hurry up, Mrs. Gallup, let him in.

MRS. GALLUP. *(Sourly entering from kitchen)* I declare, that Finnegan smells out our dinners from all the way across town. *(She opens front door with a weary jerk.)*

(FINNEGAN *enters. He is a dainty, natty little Irishman*

about Patrick's age. He wears a check suit, gray derby, yellow gloves and carries a cane. Everything about FINNEGAN *exudes a twinkle. He has the cocky charm of a song and dance man, which he actually was. His speech is more Irish than* PATRICK'S.)

FINNEGAN. Good afternoon to you, Mrs. Gallup.

PATRICK. Come in, you old rascal!

FINNEGAN. Hello, Patrick.

PATRICK. *(As they shake hands warmly)* It's been a dog's age.

MRS. GALLUP. *(Crossing down Left above chaise— weary conviction in her voice)* You'll stay to dinner of course, Mr. Finnegan?

FINNEGAN. Mrs. Gallup, the pressure of your hospitality I cannot resist.

(MRS. GALLUP *exits into kitchen.)*

PATRICK. Tell me now, Finnegan, where the devil have you been? I stopped in the haberdashery shop the other day and they said you were away. Where have you been keeping yourself?

FINNEGAN. I haven't been keeping myself—I've been kept.

PATRICK. What the devil do you mean?

FINNEGAN. *(Sits Left of table)* Ah, Patrick, I'd rather not say. I don't want to burden you with my miseries.

PATRICK. *(Right of table)* Nonsense—tell me.

FINNEGAN. No, no. I'll not darken your day with my problems.

PATRICK. Your problems are mine—what's a friend for? Now speak up, Finnegan! What's your trouble?

FINNEGAN. Well—if you insist. Patrick, the ex-Mrs. Finnegan has at last committed the ultimate infamy.

PATRICK. Good God, man, what's she done now?

FINNEGAN. *(Who relishes the telling of his miseries)* You may well ask that. Sit down and brace yourself for a shock.

(PATRICK *sits Morris chair.*)

(FINNEGAN, *the story teller, takes over*) I am coming out of the haberdashery shop a week ago, my thin pay check in my pocket—twenty-five measly, underfed dollars. And who is waiting to pounce? Her Highness, the Harpie, herself. There she stands, the former rolling pin, jaws dripping to taste my blood. "Where's my alimony," she says. I look at her. I *just look* at her! (FINNEGAN *pauses to outstare the imaginary Harpie*) "Ex Mrs. Finnegan," I says. "In the words of the immortal bard— go to hell!"

PATRICK. A place too good for her! Continue!

FINNEGAN. She holds out her claw. "My alimony," she says, "or I call a cop!" I look at her. I *just look* at her! *(Again he illustrates his contempt with a look)* "Go ahead," I says, *"call* a cop!"

(Pause. FINNEGAN *holds a pose of contempt.)*

PATRICK. *(Impatient)* What happened?

FINNEGAN. She called a cop. I was put in the pokey for a week.

PATRICK. What! Oh Finnegan—jailed! A man like yourself! Why, that unspeakable woman! *(He considers a moment in horror; rises; crosses Right)* Well, I warned you, remember. I warned you the very day you blundered into the church. Now, ten years later you're reaping the harvest.

FINNEGAN. I know. I'll never understand how she managed to hook me. I wasn't even drunk at the time!

PATRICK. The answer is tragically simple, my friend. You were seduced by virtue.

FINNEGAN. *(Puzzled)* By virtue of what?

PATRICK. *(Crosses to Right of Morris chair)* Simply by virtue! You were a song and dance man in your youth. You were surrounded by ladies of—shall I say—*un*-easy virtue. You never knew what is called a "good woman" till you met Mrs. Finnegan.

FINNEGAN. Aye! There you have it! There is nothing

to undermine a man like a good woman, and a librarian into the bargain.

PATRICK. So what naturally followed— Steeped as you were in soiled womanhood—that Harpie's damn chastity led you astray! You were seduced by her primness. Raped by her propriety.

FINNEGAN. In short, I lost my bachelorhood. *(Reflects)* Ah, what a beast she was!

PATRICK. *(Sits Morris chair)* And still is, may I add. Well, what are you going to do?

FINNEGAN. *(Rises; crosses Left)* I don't know.

PATRICK. You're not going to go on paying her? She has money!

FINNEGAN. *(Below chaise. Banging his cane for emphasis)* On my dead body the vulture can feed, but no living Finnegan pays her again.

PATRICK. That's the way to talk! She should get nothing on principle!

FINNEGAN. *(At bar)* Nothing is what I've been giving her on principle!

PATRICK. *(Becoming thoughtful)* On the other hand, you can't go bouncing in and out of jail forever either— Ah, she's a difficult problem. If only she'd marry again—

FINNEGAN. *(Drinks. Crosses down)* A prospective suitor for the hand of the ex-Mrs. Finnegan must have three outstanding qualifications; he must be deaf, dumb and blind.

PATRICK. You married her once, I hate to remind you.

FINNEGAN. *(Sits chair)* Ah yes, but years ago—before the old raisin dried up.

PATRICK. She was no grape even then. *(He thinks)* Now let's see. Let's—let's clarify the problem. We start with two basic facts. One—you will not go to jail again. Right?

FINNEGAN. Right!

PATRICK. Two, you will not pay her alimony again. Right?

FINNEGAN. Right!

PATRICK. Now—all we have to do is reconcile. *(He thinks.)*

(FINNEGAN *pretends to think, eyeing him.*)
Strategy, Finnegan, strategy. We must out-maneuver this
woman with strategy. *(Rises; crosses down.)*

FINNEGAN. *(Seemingly struck with a new idea—rises)*
Patrick, I have it!

PATRICK. Oh? What's your plan of action?

FINNEGAN. Simplicity itself. My plan of action is—
inaction!

PATRICK. Explain that.

FINNEGAN. Just that. I quit my job. I cease to produce.
I've drawn my last pay check. As long as the Harpie continues her activities, I block them—by suspended anima-
tion.

PATRICK. *(Crosses to* FINNEGAN) By Jupiter you're
right! Why of course! What did Thomas Jefferson do
when he was persecuted by his political enemies?

FINNEGAN. What?

PATRICK. Nothing! Absolutely nothing! He just *sat!*
Finally his enemies fell apart under the strain.

FINNEGAN. *(Sits)* Did they now?

PATRICK. *(Sits Left of table)* That's it, Finnegan. You
quit! Get the boss to fire you. That way she can't jail you
and she can't take your money.

FINNEGAN. Precisely! She cannot get blood from a
stone and she cannot get blood from a stone-broke Finnegan!

PATRICK. Right! *(His face begins to cloud a little.)*

FINNEGAN. *(Shakes hands)* Right!

PATRICK. Wait a bit, though. There's a flaw here somewhere—

FINNEGAN. Well, it's true, I've not worked out all the
angles.

PATRICK. For example, how do you survive?

FINNEGAN. Ah, Patrick, you've a powerful mind for
details. Yes, indeed—the question is—how do I eat—and
drink? *(He glances suggestively at kitchen door.)*

PATRICK. Ah, what's the matter with me. Why that's
easily solved! Why you can eat right here with us!

FINNEGAN. Oh, Patrick, I wouldn't dream of imposing—!

PATRICK. Nonsense, Finnegan!

FINNEGAN. Well—if you insist.

(They rise and shake hands.)

Ah—Patrick. One more little thing.

PATRICK. What?

FINNEGAN. Where do I lay my head?

PATRICK. What?

FINNEGAN. Where do I sleep? I'll have to give up my room.

PATRICK. *(Crossing down Right)* Damnit all, let me think. Well, you'd be welcome here but all our rooms are full.

(With his cane FINNEGAN *suggestively parts curtains of alcove, then walks away innocently.)*

See here now, we'll not be stopped for want of a little space! Don't you know someone who— *(He is now above the table.)*

FINNEGAN. *(Right of alcove, shakes head)* Not for any extended period.

PATRICK. I'll inquire around. I'll think of some friend who'll oblige. *(He is pacing. He stops by the now open curtains. The sight of the open alcove gives him the idea that* FINNEGAN *had intended)* Finnegan!

FINNEGAN. Hum?

PATRICK. Could you stand it in there?

FINNEGAN. *(Innocently)* Where?

PATRICK. In there. We can fix the couch as a bed—

FINNEGAN. Oh no! I couldn't think of that!

PATRICK. Of course you can.

(He and FINNEGAN *shake hands.)*

FINNEGAN. Well, if you insist. Ah, Patrick, you're a real friend!

PATRICK. It's nothing at all, my dear Finnegan. Nothing at all. Glad to have you around. You're a man to cheer up the devil himself. Oh now—I must first bring this matter up before the family council.

FINNEGAN. *(Crosses Right of table, worried by this development)* The council? Couldn't we bypass the council?

PATRICK. No. No. Finnegan. You know how important I hold my family council to be. I run this house democratically.

FINNEGAN. In this case, why can't you just put your foot down and tell the girls I'm staying. It's safer. *(Sits Left arm of Morris chair.)*

PATRICK. No, Finnegan. I'd be taking away their rights. In the old country I spent two years in jail for speaking my mind and asking my rights. And I want no smallest stain of oppression like that ever to touch my girls. They must be free—and without fear.

FINNEGAN. You've no worry there. They're certainly perky and independent enough.

PATRICK. *(A laugh of pleasure and pride)* Aye—that they are. And I'm proud of them for it. They stand on their own two feet and fight for their rights—all thanks to my family council. So I can not bypass it on this or anything else.

FINNEGAN. But, Patrick, the girls might object.

PATRICK. *(Crosses, front of table)* In general, I find it very difficult for four young girls to agree on anything but sometimes for the good of the whole I find it necessary to sway the votes of one of the little ones.

(ROSALIE *and* RITA *enter from kitchen; cross to down Left Center.)*

(PATRICK *crosses below table. Picks* GIRLS *up, twirls)* Well, look who's here!

RITA. Papa's home! Hello, Papa.

ROSALIE. Hello, Papa.

FINNEGAN. *(Below chair)* Good afternoon, ladies.

GIRLS. Hello, Mr. Finnegan.

PATRICK. Well, well, how are my two physicians. Did you treat any patients today?

ROSALIE. Oh, yes, Papa.

RITA. Oh, yes we did.

FINNEGAN. *(Crosses up)* Well, I'll be running along for the moment, Patrick.

(GIRLS *cross up.*)

PATRICK. Don't be late for supper, Finnegan.

FINNEGAN. *(On level)* Supper is one thing I never keep waiting. *(To little* GIRLS*)* Goodbye, ladies. If you're still in a medical mood when I return I will allow you to remove my appendix. *(He gives* PATRICK *a wink, then thumbs up.)*

GIRLS. Oh gee, thanks.

FINNEGAN. Not at all. Up, Thomas Jefferson!

PATRICK. Up!

(Exit FINNEGAN *front door.)*

(PATRICK *is between* GIRLS *above the table)* Ah, wouldn't it be nice to have Finnegan living with us. Then you could operate on him day after day. Here, Doctors, I brought you a present. It's a bit of real medical equipment. *(Takes stethoscope from briefcase.)*

ROSALIE. A real one, Rita.

RITA. Gee, Papa, thanks. *(She takes stethoscope.)*

PATRICK. Do you know what it's called?

ROSALIE. Of course we know, Papa!

RITA. It's a stethoscope—we know *that!*

PATRICK. That's right. You know how to use it? Remember what Doctor Foster does with it?

ROSALIE. Yes, Papa, I know. You listen to the heart.

PATRICK. Well, let's see you use it then.

RITA. Will you be our patient, Papa?

PATRICK. *(Crosses to chaise and sits in reclining position)* Am I not always?

RITA. *(Getting hold of stethoscope. Left of chaise)* Let me try it first!

ROSALIE. *(Right of chaise)* No, *I* want to!

PATRICK. Now, now, Doctors—one at a time. Rita, you start the examination. Rosalie—you are the specialist— you will be called in later.

ROSALIE. Oh! All right then.

RITA. *(Placing the stethoscope considerably below his heart and listening eagerly)* I hear something, Papa! It goes Burp— Burp— Burp.

PATRICK. My heart's up here. Up here. *(He moves stethoscope to proper position)* There. Now hear it?

RITA. Gee! Listen to that!

PATRICK. Let the specialist hear it.

(GIRLS *switch positions.*)

Now Rita, you be the nurse. You take my pulse.

ROSALIE. *(Taking her turn at listening, Left of him)* Gosh. It booms. Boom! Boom! Boom!

PATRICK. And what is the heart doing when it makes that sound?

RITA. It's beating, Papa.

PATRICK. Yes, but what for? What's all the beating about?

(They are BOTH *blank for a moment.)*

I trust our specialist knows the answer to that? What's on top of the well in our yard?

ROSALIE. A pump! It's like a pump. Only the heart pumps blood!

PATRICK. Right you are, Doctor Rosalie. But my heart is a much finer pump than the one on our well. This ingenious little pump here goes on pumping day after day, year after year, and never stops till I die.

RITA. Oh, please don't die, Papa! Never!

ROSALIE. You're never going to really die are you, Papa?

PATRICK. *(Laughs)* I've absolutely no intention of dying. Why should I? With two fine doctors like yourselves to take care of me! *(With one arm around each he hugs them)* And now I think you've examined your patient enough for the moment. Rita, run upstairs and tell your sisters to come down. I wish a brief meeting of the family council.

RITA. *(Taking stethoscope)* All right, Papa. *(She runs off upstairs.)*

PATRICK. *(Sitting* ROSALIE *down on chaise)* By the way,

Rosalie, Mr. Finnegan's an old friend of mine, as you know. I'm planning to have him live with us for a while—if the family council approves of course.

ROSALIE. But—where would he stay, Papa?

PATRICK. *(Indicating alcove)* In there.

ROSALIE. *(Rises; crosses to Left Center)* Gosh—right there?

PATRICK. Your other sisters may object, I know.

ROSALIE. *(Worriedly—looking at alcove again)* Oh, gee, Papa— We keep our ambulance in there.

PATRICK. Ah, by the way, Rosalie—I had something, something especially for you and I went and forgot to bring it home with me.

ROSALIE. *(To Right of him)* Something for me, Papa? What?

PATRICK. Just a whole box of chocolate creams, that's all. I must have left it on my desk.

ROSALIE. A whole box, just for me! Oh, Papa.

PATRICK. Shhh! A pound of the most delectable confectionary in the world. So I hope you'll *be* loyal to Mr. Finnegan and to your father too.

ROSALIE. Oh, thank you, Papa. *(She kisses him.)*

(He hears GIRLS *coming and goes "Shhh!" to* ROSALIE. MAGGIE *and* MARY *come downstairs with* RITA.*)*

PATRICK. I'll remember to bring it tomorrow.

MAGGIE. You want a meeting of the family council, Papa? What for?

PATRICK. I have a small matter to bring up. Sit down, it won't take long.

(With an air of businesslike seriousness the GIRLS *take their seats.* MARY *gets a notebook from table.)*

Now let's see. Who's supposed to be chairman today?

MARY. *(Checking in notebook)* It's Rita's turn.

PATRICK. Very well, Rita—take over.

RITA. *(Pounding gavel)* Yes, Papa. Meeting come to order!

PATRICK. You are not mending the woodshed. You have our attention already, darling. Proceed!

RITA. Yes, Papa. Will the secretary please read the minutes of the last meeting.

MARY. *(Rises, clears throat and reads from notebook)* "August sixth, nineteen hundred and twelve. Under the rotating system, Maggie was chairman. The treasurer was asked to kive her report and Rosalie said that there was eighteen cents left in the treasury. It was unanimously voted to raise new funds by the usual method and Papa gave the treasurer five dollars. Under new business Papa raised the question of grasshoppers in the preserve jars, and a vote of censure was taken against Rita and Rosalie. The vote was seventy-eight against grasshoppers, seventeen for." *(Sits.)*

PATRICK. *(Rises)* Madam Chairman, speaking of grasshoppers I should like to say a word or two on garter snakes—

RITA. *(Pounds gavel)* The chair recognizes Papa.

PATRICK. *(Above Morris chair)* Thank you. When we voted to censure grasshoppers, it was not the sense of this meeting to open the door to garter snakes. The point seems to have been missed by you, Madam Chairman, and by Rosalie. The point is—nothing goes in the preserve jars except preserves.

ROSALIE. *(On footstool)* I think the point is well taken, don't you, Rita?

RITA. Shall we amend the minutes to make that clear, Papa?

PATRICK. That won't be necessary—just so the issue is clear in your minds. *(He looks rather sternly at ROSA-LIE and RITA. Sits.)*

RITA. Oh yes, Papa—you've made it perfectly clear now.

PATRICK. Very well. Then I move the minutes be accepted.

MAGGIE. Second.

RITA. All in favor say "aye."

ALL. Aye.

RITA. *(Pounds)* Is there some new business, Papa?

PATRICK. Yes. *(Rises.)*

RITA. The chair recognizes Papa.

PATRICK. Thank you. Madam Chairman, I have a grave matter for the council's consideration— *(To above Morris chair)* My childhood friend, Leonard Francis Finnegan, finds himself in grievous straits due to the maneuvers of the ex-Mrs. Finnegan.

ROSALIE. What are maneuvers?

PATRICK. Tricks, Rosalie, dirty tricks. I shall omit the tragic details. It is not my purpose to parade Finnegan's misery before the world. Suffice to say that he finds himself in need of a friend's helping hand. In order to parry the vindictive blows of the ex-Mrs. Finnegan, it becomes wise, in fact strategically necessary, for Mr. Finnegan to stay here with us for a while—as our guest.

MAGGIE. Good Lord! Papa! We're crowded now!

MARY. Where could he stay?

ROSALIE. Does he have to hide, Papa?

RITA. *(Pounding gavel)* The meeting will come to order. Continue, Papa.

PATRICK. I therefore move that Mr. Finnegan be taken into our home until further notice.

MAGGIE. Oh, *no,* Papa. There's just no room!

MARY. We'd never get into the bathroom!

PATRICK. *(To* ALL*)* Does anybody second my motion? *(They* ALL *turn away.)*

(To ROSALIE, *Right of chair)* Does anybody second my motion? *(He pulls one of her pigtails secretively.)*

ROSALIE. *(Rises)* I second the motion.

MAGGIE. What's the matter with you, Rosalie. Why?

PATRICK. *(Righteous)* Don't intimidate a voter, Maggie.

MAGGIE. *(Rises)* Papa, I'm sure we all like Mr. Finnegan but—well, just for one thing—where could he sleep?

PATRICK. *(Crosses Left—indicating alcove)* He has expressed a willingness to accept that simple cubicle as his home.

MAGGIE. *(Steps up)* In *there?* But that's awful! This is our *living* room!

PATRICK. Well, he'll be living in it.

MARY. What happens to privacy, Papa?

PATRICK. Those humble curtains will suffice him.

MARY. Our privacy, I mean! If he moves here he'll eat us out of house and home.

PATRICK. *(Crosses down. Sits)* Irrelevant and immaterial. He does anyway.

MAGGIE. *(To* ROSALIE*)* You realize, don't you, Rosalie, that you and Rita will have to move all your old toys out of the room—

ROSALIE. *(Rises, crosses to Left of* PATRICK*)* Oh, Papa, will we have to do *that?*

PATRICK. *(Arm around* ROSALIE, *pats her stomach)* Rosalie, I'm sure is above such petty thoughts. She has her mind on higher considerations. Now let's not argue this thing all night. Rita, close the discussion and come to the vote.

MAGGIE. Now just a minute, Papa. *(Rises)* I can't see the wisdom of Finnegan cluttering up our living room, and I'd like to see us four girls stick together for once and vote this down.

PATRICK. Maggie Flannigan, where's your hospitality. Just you wait 'til sometime when *you* want—

MAGGIE. You're threatening a voter, Papa.

MARY. That was a threat, Papa. Pay the fine.

PATRICK. I was not threatening. I was merely pointing out—

RITA. *(Pounds)* Pay the fine, Papa.

MAGGIE. *(Sits)* I'm sorry, Papa, but you've always said we should speak and vote our own minds in this council.

PATRICK. So I have. And let's get on with the vote.

RITA. It has been moved and seconded that Mr. Finnegan be allowed—

PATRICK. Not "allowed"—"invited."

RITA. Invited to come and live with us. We will proceed to vote in the usual manner. Maggie?

MAGGIE. Seventeen votes—no.

MARY. Sixteen votes—no.

RITA. Seven votes—no.

ROSALIE. Ten votes—yes.

RITA. Papa?

PATRICK. I cast forty-five votes—yes.

RITA. Motion carried. *(She pounds the gavel.)*

(ROSALIE *crosses back to her footstool.)*

PATRICK. *(Rising)* May I have the floor, Madame Chairman?

RITA. Yes, Papa.

PATRICK. Now that the council, in its wisdom, has decided in favor of admitting Mr. Finnegan to our family group, I should like to suggest that in the interest of politeness—and simple hospitality—the record be amended to read that the vote was unanimous.

MAGGIE. Why not, Papa? I'll second that motion.

RITA. *(Pounds)* All in favor say "aye."

ALL. Aye.

PATRICK. Good. And now I move the meeting be adjourned.

RITA. All in favor?

ALL. Aye.

(MAGGIE *and* RITA *return chair, gavel, etc., to desk down Right.* MARY *chair to arch Right.)*

PATRICK. All right, Madam Chairman, you and Rosalie run along and clean up for dinner.

(Sound of HURDY GURDY.)

MARY. *(Above table)* Hum! Whichever way Papa votes it's practically unanimous.

PATRICK. *(Sits Morris chair)* Well, that's the reward of age, Mary. Someday you'll command as many votes as I do now. Now let's see, where's my paper?

ROSALIE. *(Who has been waiting her opportunity)* Here, Papa. *(Hands* PATRICK *paper.)*

PATRICK. Thank you, darling.

ROSALIE. *(Softly)* A whole pound of chocolates, Papa.

PATRICK. Hum? Oh, yes, yes.

ROSALIE. Come on, Rita. Let's play doctor.

RITA. All right, I'll be the nurse.

(The Two *of them run off upstairs. Outside, the hurdy gurdy MUSIC swells.)*

PATRICK. That was one of your mother's favorite tunes. You know, Maggie, you grow more like her every day.

MAGGIE. *(Sitting chaise)* Do I, Papa. Thank you.

PATRICK. She was a wonderful woman.

MARY. *(Who has been lighting the gas lights)* Mama was very young when you got married, wasn't she?

PATRICK. *(Buried in paper)* Yes.

MARY. *(Crosses to sit Left of table)* Papa, I've been thinking—

PATRICK. A very worthwhile activity.

MARY. Papa—suppose I decided to give up my career?

PATRICK. *(Still half in his paper)* What career? What do you mean?

MARY. My career on the stage.

PATRICK. How can you give that up when you haven't even begun yet?

MARY. I mean I've given up the idea of it.

PATRICK. *(Mild interest, still half in newspaper)* That so?

MARY. Would you mind if I should change my career to marriage, Papa?

PATRICK. *(Still on intellectual level and half in his paper)* Mind? Of course not. My position has always been that all careers should be open to women. But if marriage is what you want, then by Jupiter you get married.

MARY. You really approve, Papa! *(Rises, crosses behind* PATRICK, *kisses him, then to footstool and sits.)*

(MAGGIE to sit Left of table.)

Oh, Papa, you're wonderful! Maggie, did you hear what he said?

PATRICK. What? Wait a minute— *(He puts down his paper for first time)* Why am I so wonderful? What do you mean?

MARY. To let us get married! Oh, Papa!

PATRICK. *(Shocked)* You mean—*now!*

MARY. Well, fairly soon anyway. Why not?

PATRICK. Why *not!* In the first place you've got school and college to finish. What nonsense is this? Marriage at your age!

MARY. I'm going on seventeen.

PATRICK. Well, the voyage has just started. You're sixteen years and one month.

MARY. But when I finally pick the right one—we can get married, can't we? I mean with your consent.

PATRICK. When and if you finally pick the right man, Daughter, and the time is right and your educational problems have been taken care of then—then we'll see—

MAGGIE. Papa, did it ever occur to you that maybe you exaggerate the importance of college education a little?

PATRICK. No it did not!

MAGGIE. You've often said that life itself is a school.

PATRICK. A school maybe—but not a college. What on earth are you driving at, Maggie? Why are *you*—

MAGGIE. I'm just wondering about the whole question of college. Now look at Mr. Tollman down the road. He went to Harvard, and you've always said he's the biggest fool on Kinsman Road.

PATRICK. Which only proves that even Harvard cannot make a man of a jackass.

MAGGIE. You didn't go to college at all but you know lots more than Mr. Tollman.

PATRICK. I do not! *(Backs up quickly)* Well, that is— yes, damn it, I do. But I've educated myself.

MAGGIE. And how much better to do it your way perhaps. You lived while you learned. Maybe Mary would rather educate herself—like you did. And get married.

MARY. Yes, Maggie, I would!

PATRICK. Well, you won't!

MAGGIE. By the time she finished college she'd be an old maid!

PATRICK. Old maid—! At twenty-one—?

MAGGIE. You have absolutely no sense of reality sometimes.

PATRICK. I haven't—? You sit there and tell me she'll be an old maid at twenty-one! And you say *I* have no sense of reality!

MAGGIE. Papa, almost all girls that age have husbands.

PATRICK. Almost all dogs have fleas! Is that to say that fleas are desirable?

(FINNEGAN's *special KNOCK on door.*)

Well, that's Finnegan. Let's discuss it later. *(He rises to go to door)* By the way—remember. The vote was unanimous.

MARY. It was not, Papa.

PATRICK. The final one was— *(Calls upstairs)* Rita! Rosalie! Come down! *(To* MAGGIE *and* MARY*)* So greet him with the proper joy, mind you. *(He opens the door.)*

(FINNEGAN *steps in.*)

Welcome back, Finnegan!

FINNEGAN. Thank you, Patrick. *(To* RITA *and* ROSALIE *as they come downstairs)* Again, good afternoon, ladies. *(Enters living room, greets* MAGGIE *and* MARY *who cross to chaise)* Ah, and how are the two eldest flowers of the Flannigan garden?

(MAGGIE *and* MARY *sit on chaise.*)

MAGGIE *and* MARY. Good afternoon, Mr. Finnegan.

PATRICK. Sit down, Finnegan—and make yourself *truly* at home.

FINNEGAN. Ah—thank you, Patrick. Could that mean—

PATRICK. Yes, Finnegan, I think you'll be happy to learn that the family council has unanimously—and *enthusiastically* voted for you to live with us.

FINNEGAN. *(Puts bag down. Courteous surprise)* What

a charming surprise! Thank you, ladies, from the bottom of my heart. You're angels all of you.

MARY. What has the ex-Mrs. Finnegan done now, Mr. Finnegan?

FINNEGAN. *(Sits Left of table)* What has happened now, Mary, is simply this. She has reduced me to penury. She has forced me against my will and contrary to all my principles to take refuge here and reluctantly accept the bounty of your father.

MARY. How long are you planning to stay—

FINNEGAN. Well—just at the moment my plans are indefinite.

ROSALIE. You're staying indefinitely?

FINNEGAN. Well—that's rather a long word. Oh, Patrick, here's a special delivery letter the postman handed me as I came up the path.

PATRICK. *(Takes letter)* Thank you.

FINNEGAN. *(Taking apple from bowl on table)* May I?

MAGGIE. Of course.

FINNEGAN. On second thought—later. Why spoil a delicious supper.

PATRICK. *(Rises)* Maggie! It's come! From Vassar! And bless your heart, child, you're accepted!

(GIRLS *rise—"hooray."*)

FINNEGAN. *(Rises and crosses to sideboard and back to table, bringing wine and glasses)* This calls for a celebration. We must drink a toast to Maggie.

PATRICK. *(Crosses to MAGGIE)* Ah, this is a red letter day for the house of Flannigan! *(Gives MAGGIE letter)* Rita, Rosalie, you shall have your first taste of wine. *(Crosses to above table.)*

(FINNEGAN *pours wine.*)

RITA. Real wine?

ROSALIE. Gosh, thanks, Papa! Thanks!

PATRICK. *(Giving little ones glasses)* There now. Stay sober.

ROSALIE. You like wine, don't you, Mr. Finnegan?

FINNEGAN. *(Crosses to give wine to* MARY *and* MAGGIE*)* Frankly, Rosalie, I have always preferred the grain to the grape.

RITA. *(Realizing glass is almost empty)* Aw, Mr. Finnegan, you didn't put in any at all!

PATRICK. He certainly did. Enough for a toast.

ROSALIE. But Papa, you said we could taste it.

PATRICK. And so you can. That's a taste. *(To* FINNEGAN*)* What do you say? As the oldest friend and newest member of the Flannigan family, I think we should give Finnegan the honor of offering the first toast!

FINNEGAN. Ah, Patrick—I fear I'm a skeleton at this feast.

PATRICK. Nonsense, man! Speak up! Quiet, all. Finnegan will make the first toast!

FINNEGAN. *(Left Center)* Well, if you insist—ahem. Patrick—ladies. I'm afraid I feel just a mite out of key with proceedings but—well, as you know I have never completely shared your father's enthusiasm for educating the ladies. Even in their uncultivated state they pose such a major problem that I tremble to think what may happen when they add learning to their arsenal—

PATRICK. *(Good-naturedly)* Ah, Finnegan, you're incorrigible—

FINNEGAN. However. In the case of these four angelic exceptions—I am sure nothing but good can come of it. Therefore—my sincere congratulations, Maggie.

PATRICK. From the bottom of our hearts, child!

(They ALL *drink.)*

And now I'll make the toast! To the first Flannigan who will ever see a college!

(They start to drink.)

Now wait a minute, wait! I'm not finished yet! I have something to say. You'd better all sit down. (PATRICK *crosses down Center.)*

(FINNEGAN *crosses down Left of chaise.* ROSALIE *sits footstool.* RITA *sits Morris chair.)*

It's as well, my children, that you don't even know what a long road it's been to this hour. A road that's wound up from the soil of Ireland and from ignorance as black as night. But I brought with me knowledge of evil things which are only words to you girls. You do not know poverty because I knew it. *(Crosses up)* You do not know tyranny because I knew it. You do not know ignorance because I knew it. And I swore to lift myself and my own forever out of the dust. I've had no college; but I've scavenged knowledge along life's way that gave me the strength to wash the dirt from my hands, and build this home and live in dignity. *(Above table)* What you must do is much more. You're women—or will be, and even here you've a battle ahead to win full lives for yourselves. Much of the world says you're cows to be put out to breed as soon as your bodies are ripe. But the truth is you're human beings with every right to live as richly as men! And your chance for that life lies in knowledge. What little I know I try to pass on to you, but there's more to learn than I have to teach. Today the first one of you—our Maggie—begins her climb above me. And each of you will follow in turn. *(To* MAGGIE *directly—crosses to Center)* I can only say, child, that I'm proud as a king to think that it's up from my shoulder you're stepping. Let us drink to our Maggie! *(Holds glass high for toast)* May the knowledge of truth light all of your years, and your thirst for it never be quenched!

(ALL *drink.* MAGGIE *is about to burst into tears.)* Why, child, what's the matter?

MAGGIE. *(Rises)* Papa—I—I don't want to hurt you but I— *(She can't go on.)*

PATRICK. Hurt me! Why today's the day you've made me the happiest!

MAGGIE. I know—forgive me, I—I'm just crying that's all— *(Exits upstairs.)*

PATRICK. *(Crosses up stage)* Can you beat it, Finnegan? A happy occasion and she floods us with tears!

FINNEGAN. *(Left of* PATRICK*)* As I've always said, Patrick, an inscrutable species.

CURTAIN

ACT TWO

Curtain Rises *on empty stage. There is a TAP and then*
Finnegan enters, much more dapper than usual be-
cause he has a few drinks under his belt. He twirls
his cane in his gloved hand and, hat still on, enters
the living room. He is humming "Tavern in the
Town." Seeing no one present, he crosses down Right,
twirling his cane and doing a dance step on the way.

Finnegan. *(To tune of "Tavern in the Town")*
I'm a lily of the field! Of the field
I toil not neither do I spin, no indeed!
But I go all day without a stroke of work
Fare thee well, fare thee well, fare thee welllll!

(He pauses to examine his jaunty self in the mirror. He
finds himself pleasing to himself. He turns as he hears
a rumpus of small feet on the stairs. Rita and
Rosalie run down in search of something.)

Rosalie. I'll get it, Rita. I said *I'll* get it! I know
where it is!

Rita. *(Crosses to chaise)* So do I and I want to take it
to Papa.

Finnegan. *(Crosses to above table as they enter the*
living room) Well, ladies, and what is the meaning of all
this excitement?

Rosalie. *(Crosses to Finnegan above Morris chair)*
Papa is sick up in the playroom!

Finnegan. *(Shocked)* What!

Rita. *(Crosses to Left Center)* And we forgot the ambulance!

31

FINNEGAN. Oh, I see—

RITA. *(Fighting with* ROSALIE *over the ambulance)* Let *me* have it! Rosalie, let go!

FINNEGAN. Ah, what a fortunate man is your father, to have two such charming handmaidens in attendance.

ROSALIE. *(Crosses to above* FINNEGAN*)* Mr. Finnegan, are you drunk?

FINNEGAN. Let us never use that offensive word. Let us say that I am—as the French have it—un peu parti—a little departed.

ROSALIE. *(Above table Right)* A little departed?

RITA. *(Above table Left)* But you're still here!

FINNEGAN. Ah, but not all here! In my present state, I see the panorama of life with *less* confusion than those whose minds are befuddled with sobriety.

ROSALIE. Mrs. Burton's husband drinks a lot too, and Papa's always telling him drinking's bad for you.

FINNEGAN. I wouldn't want to contradict your father but what he undoubtedly meant was—drinking is bad for Mr. Burton. With me it's different. With me it unlocks the sleeping spirit, thaws my talents—frozen by unemployment and reminds me that I am still a song and dance man in my heart—

(He places his derby over his heart and goes into a song and dance while the little GIRLS *watch delightedly, particularly when* FINNEGAN *falls over a hassock— then sits on hassock. From on high comes the voice of* PATRICK*.)*

PATRICK. *(Off)* Doctors! Hey there, Doctors! If you don't bring that ambulance I'll be well in a minute.

ROSALIE. *(Crosses down)* We've got to go, Mr. Finnegan. Papa's badly hurt.

FINNEGAN. He is! Well, that's two of us.

ROSALIE. Will you do that again for us sometime?

FINNEGAN. Any time, ladies. Any time at all.

ROSALIE. Oh, thank you. *(Exit* ROSALIE *upstairs.)*

Rita. *(Lingering a moment after* Rosalie *starts off)* By—

Finnegan. *(Taking her hand and kissing it in the grand manner)* Goodbye, lovely lady. Ah, lucky, lucky invalid—your father.

(Shy and charmed, Rita *runs off upstairs after her sister.)*

(Alone, Finnegan *crosses to sideboard to sneak a drink, singing as he goes)*

"Chase your father up a tree
With a large shillelagh
Put your mother on the wall
With a pretty cannon ball."

(Drinks)

"I'm a lily of the field, of the field!
I toil not, neither do I spin!"

(Meanwhile the front door opens and Mrs. Gallup *enters, staggering under a huge load of groceries that all but obscures her face. She has a deal of trouble maneuvering them.)*

Madame seems to be somewhat encumbered.

Mrs. Gallup. Oh, dear. How am I ever going to get to the kitchen with all this?

Finnegan. *(Suddenly makes a quick, sweeping turn and walks rapidly to* Mrs. Gallup*)* At your service, Princess! *(With breathtaking speed he picks up* Mrs. Gallup *by the legs, packages and all, straight in the air. Carrying her thus, like the grocery laden figure head a a ship, he crosses the room and swiftly deposits her at the kitchen door. He doffs his derby with a flourish, opens the door and bows)* Madame, you are *at* the kitchen! If I can ever be of service again, don't hesitate to call on me! *(He clamps his derby back on his head and walks with dignity into his alcove.)*

(Uttering no sound, Mrs. Gallup *continues to stand where he set her down, the packages still obscuring her face from view.* Mary *appears at the door.)*

MARY. *(Down Left)* My Lord, Mrs. Gallup. How did you carry all these? Here, let me help you. *(She takes the top packages away, revealing* MRS. GALLUP'S *face once more. Busy with the packages, she does not notice* MRS. GALLUP'S *wide-eyed, stunned expression. She disappears with some of the packages into the kitchen.)*

MRS. GALLUP. *(Her lips moving in a mystic whisper)*
When and where you least expect it
Comes a man who's strong and brave—
To carry you and all your burdens—
Forever after—till the grave.

(She crosses the living room on this and heads up the stairs. At this moment PATRICK *comes down.)*

PATRICK. Oh, hello, Mrs. Gallup.
   (Enter MARY.*)*
Is there anything the matter?

*(*MRS. GALLUP *goes upstairs, unhearing.)*

MARY. *(Crossing Right)* I guess she was carrying too big a load. *(She exits into kitchen with other packages; re-enters immediately; crosses Right, below table, to window.)*

PATRICK. *(Right of Morris chair—with a glance at* MARY, *who is dressed up)* Well, you're looking very pretty today, Mary. Is this for Mr. Penrose's benefit?

MARY. *(At window)* Not especially, Papa.

PATRICK. *(Crosses up)* What's holding Maggie up? She's been in her room for two hours.

MARY. She's just dressing, Papa. It takes time.

PATRICK. *(To Right of Morris chair)* More time than usual today, I'd say. Ahem—Mary—your sister seems quite interested in this Penrose boy, doesn't she? Has she said anything about him to you?

MARY. I believe I heard her say she thinks he's heavenly.

PATRICK. Hmmm—heavenly. *(Crosses to down Center.)*

MARY. What are you worried about, Papa? Are you afraid Maggie's going to run off and get married?

PATRICK. *(Right of chaise)* Married! No, I am not afraid of that—because she is under age and requires my consent.

MARY. Oh. You mean—you wouldn't let her? No matter how nice he is?

PATRICK. I mean exactly that. *(Crosses up to bottom of stairs)* To all whom it may concern, be it known that there'll be no marriages around here while people are still in their swaddling clothes! After college, is another matter. *(Clears throat, pauses, returning into the room, goes to MARY down Right)* You may convey that information to any interested parties, Mary. It may save considerable embarrassment. *(Sits chair Right.)*

(MAGGIE rushes downstairs, her dress without its belt. She hurriedly enters the living room and inspects PATRICK with disapproval.)

MAGGIE. *(Crosses to Left of his chair)* Papa, are you ready yet? I knew it! Papa, won't you please put your jacket on!

PATRICK. Well, what's the matter with this?

MAGGIE. *(Kneels Left of him)* Papa, even if this visit doesn't mean anything to you it means something to me!

PATRICK. I'm beginning to realize that.

MAGGIE. Besides, you look so handsome when you're all dressed up.

MARY. Yes, you really do, Papa. *(Crossing to Right Center.)*

PATRICK. I am not susceptible to flattery. However, in the interests of peace I'll oblige. *(He starts off.)*

MAGGIE. *(Rises)* And Papa—a white shirt.

PATRICK. *(At staircase)* The shirt stands! I'll not strip to the buff for any damn Prince of the Gas Dynasty! *(He exits upstairs.)*

MARY. *(Right of her on landing)* Papa's been trying to pump me.

MAGGIE. I know. I heard the big outburst.

MARY. His nose is out to here. He smells rats all over the place.

MAGGIE. Do you suppose he *knows* anything?

(DOORBELL rings. MARY looks out door-pane.)

MARY. *(At door)* Oh Lord, it's Ralph!

MAGGIE. You answer the door! Then come right upstairs and help me get ready quick!

MARY. All right!

(MAGGIE *runs off upstairs.* MARY *goes to door and opens to* RALPH PENROSE, *a tall, handsome young man of twenty-one or two, nervously rigid before his ordeal, dressed to kill, straw hat in one hand, bouquet in the other.)*

Oh, hello, Mr. Penrose.

RALPH. Good afternoon.

MARY. Come in—you're expected.

(RALPH *enters.*)

Excuse me. *(She runs upstairs, giggling.)*

(RALPH *looks uneasy at being left alone. He peers into the living room. Enters. Finally sits down awkwardly in chair Right, hat still in one hand, flowers in the other. He is perspiring from the strain. He sets down his hat, reaches in his pocket and pulls out his handkerchief. mops his brow. Cane in hand,* FINNEGAN *steps from his alcove.)*

FINNEGAN. *(Crosses to above table Center; stops; eyes* RALPH *appraisingly)* Good afternoon.

RALPH. *(Jumps up nervously, taken by surprise)* Oh—ah—good afternoon, sir.

FINNEGAN. *(Crossing below to Left of table)* Finnegan's the name. Friend of the family. You're Penrose, eh?

RALPH. *(Crossing)* Ah—yes, sir. How do you do? *(Shakes hands.)*

FINNEGAN. *(Sits chair Left of table, leaning forward on his cane and studying the unhappy* RALPH, *who is wiping his face again)* Won't you sit down.

RALPH. *(Sits Right of table)* Thank you, sir.

FINNEGAN. You seem warm.

RALPH. Well I—I perspire sometimes when I'm—when—

FINNEGAN. *(Nods knowingly)* I understand perfectly. Ah, you stir sad memories in my bosom.

RALPH. Beg pardon?

FINNEGAN. You took a drop of comfort before you came?

RALPH. Yes, I—how do you know? Does it show?

FINNEGAN. *(Determined to make* RALPH *even more uneasy)* Once upon a time I was even as you are now. With whiskey on my breath, perspiration on my brow and flowers in my hand. *(Shakes head with sad misgivings)* Ah, if I had only known then what I know today!

RALPH. What—what do you mean?

FINNEGAN. Young man, you're here on a very dangerous mission, or my eyes deceive me.

RALPH. Dangerous—?

FINNEGAN. Fraught with dire consequences, believe me. Who should know better than I? Ah yes, there I was, just like you—about to ask a damn—a damsel to be my bride.

RALPH. I'm asking her father.

FINNEGAN. Oh, he'll be delighted I'm sure. Anyway, it all adds up to the same thing. The same sad thing.

RALPH. Sad?

FINNEGAN. Oh, I received warnings, mind you, but I was too young and innocent to pay them heed. I size you up as a very smart young man. Yes. The advice of a completely unprejudiced observer such as myself can sometimes save a world of trouble for people.

RALPH. Well, I—ah—I don't anticipate any—great trouble, sir. Not with Maggie anyway.

FINNEGAN. *(Rises—crosses Left)* Who ever does? To the unmarried, marriage appears as a state of bliss. It is only afterwards that we discover it to be a state of siege.

RALPH. *(Also rises)* I should think, sir, that would depend on who—whom you married?

FINNEGAN. That's grammatically correct.

RALPH. Well, I—but surely you'll admit *some* marriages are alright—

FINNEGAN. That is a common error of judgment among the unmarried!

RALPH. Well, now! By George—you just can't tell me that *all* marriages are bad!

FINNEGAN. Oh, I know I can't tell you. You'll probably have to learn by experience like everyone else. But wouldn't you think that just once *somebody, somewhere, somehow* would take someone's word for it.

RALPH. You certainly have a dark view of women, sir.

FINNEGAN. Oh, women are all right in their proper place. But God forbid not in the home.

RALPH. Not in the—? Oh, now, look here, you're pulling my leg!

FINNEGAN. Look around you, my boy. Look at your own parents. I don't know them but do you often find them billing and cooing? Or do they more often just parry and thrust? *(He thrusts and his cane goes through* RALPH's *hat)* I beg your pardon. *(Wipes "blood" off cane.)*

RALPH. *(Beaten into reflection by this stab)* Well— ah—

FINNEGAN. *(Crosses Left)* Exactly! And that is the story of us all.

RALPH. George, I hope not—

FINNEGAN. Ah, but don't let me dissuade you. After all, my boy, nature has her rights and there's the next generation to be considered no matter what the cost in misery to us. Well, perhaps I should leave you. At a time such as this a man likes to be alone with his thoughts. *(Steps up.)*

RALPH. *(Steps Center. Rallying unexpectedly)* No! Now wait a minute! You've made some extraordinary statements here and—by George! I—well, I challenge them!

FINNEGAN. *(A little surprised) Do* you now? *(Crosses down.)*

RALPH. Yes. Yes, I certainly do. You see you're generalizing from your own marriage and that is *not* good logic. That is generalizing from *one* particular case.

FINNEGAN. Ah, but what a case.

RALPH. Oh, you obviously had a ghastly experience with marriage—

FINNEGAN. Oh ho! God!

RALPH. But it does not follow that all marriages are ghastly. All horses are animals but all animals are *not* horses.

FINNEGAN. *(Studies* RALPH *a moment)* Now that's a hell of a profound statement. Go on.

RALPH. I think marriage is a great institution. And what's more, I believe in human love.

FINNEGAN. *Do* you now? Well, young man, all I can say is, if you persist in these radical views there's no end to the trouble in store for you.

MAGGIE. *(Off)* Listen, you stay right here now.

(RALPH *turns Right.* MAGGIE *comes down stairs.* FINNEGAN *makes a quick decision and retires into alcove without* RALPH *noticing his departure.)*

RALPH. *(Moved by her appearance)* By George, Maggie, you look—by George!

MAGGIE. *(Left of table)* Hello, Ralph. Sorry to keep you waiting—

RALPH. Oh, that's all right. I was talking to Mr.— Where did he go? *(He looks around for* FINNEGAN.)

MAGGIE. *(Displaying her dress)* Ralph—do you like it?

RALPH. I sure do. How's your father—feeling? *(Steps in. He wants to kiss her but is shy.)*

MAGGIE. *(She would like to be kissed)* We managed to get him into a suit—that's always a good sign.

RALPH. *(Steps in)* Does he know anything yet?

MAGGIE. No, no—I want him to meet you first. *(She adjusts his handkerchief.)*

(His arm hesitates, wanting to go around her.)
Oh, you look nice—

RALPH. *(Steps in)* I had trouble with my tie again.

MAGGIE. *(A warm memory)* Remember when your tie came undone on the Ferris Wheel that time?

RALPH. George! Yes—!

MAGGIE. Oh—Cincinnati is a wonderful city—isn't it—

RALPH. It sure was—

(They start to kiss. RITA and ROSALIE come downstairs.)

RITA *and* ROSALIE. Hello, Ralphie. Did you come in your car? Are you going to take us for a ride?

RALPH. *(Crosses Right)* Hello, girls.

MAGGIE. *(Above table)* Ralph, you go ahead just as we planned. First get acquainted. Let him get over you being a Penrose, then when he starts to like you and I know he will—

RALPH. *(Nodding uneasily. To her)* Then—uh huh!

(ROSALIE *tugs at* MAGGIE.)

MAGGIE. And there's something else before Papa gets down!

RALPH. What—?

MAGGIE. Promise you'll take Rita and Rosalie for a drive two days a week for a year!

RALPH. What—?

MAGGIE. Please promise! Hurry! It's very important! Everything may depend on it!

RALPH. Twice a week for a year—

(RITA *and* ROSALIE *nod solemnly.*)

MAGGIE. Papa's coming! Please don't argue!

RALPH. Well—ah—why sure—I'd be delighted, but—

MAGGIE. *(Firmly to* RITA *and* ROSALIE) There! You heard him! He'll be delighted!

(RITA *and* ROSALIE *nod approval, cross to sit chaise.*)

RALPH. But—ah—

MAGGIE. *(Glancing upstairs, then to* RALPH) Here he comes! Courage! Papa's not half as dangerous as he seems!

(PATRICK *comes down the stairs, followed by* MARY. *He is wearing a suit. He enters the room, eyeing* RALPH *sternly. He eyes the flowers which* RALPH *has left on the Morris chair.* RALPH *picks them up nervously.*)

Papa—this is Mr. Penrose.

(MARY *up Left Center.*)

PATRICK. I'm extremely interested to meet you, Mr. Penrose. *(Crosses down.)*

RALPH. *(Below table)* I—I've been looking forward to meeting you too, sir!

(PATRICK *holds out his hand.*)

(RALPH *starts to offer his flower hand as if the flowers were for* PATRICK) These are— *(Checks himself)* Oh, that is—these are for you, Maggie— *(To* PATRICK) They're for her.

PATRICK. Why doesn't somebody relieve Mr. Penrose of his burdens?

MAGGIE. Oh, of course. Thank you, Ralph. *(She takes the flowers.)*

RALPH. Ah—thank *you.* (RALPH *shakes hands.*)

PATRICK. Do sit down, Mr. Penrose.

RALPH. Oh. Yes. Thank you.

(RALPH *starts to sit in Morris chair, but sees* GIRLS *are standing.* MAGGIE *and* MARY *sit on chaise,* MAGGIE *shooing the little ones to the footstool. As they cross they stare fixedly at* RALPH. RITA *on footstool,* ROSALIE *on Left arm of Morris chair. When all the* GIRLS *are finally seated,* RALPH *sits down. There is a long pause, during which* PATRICK *starts singing*

an indifferent chorus of "Brennan on the Moor.")
Ahem— *(Pause)* Warm—for this time of year.

PATRICK. *(Giving him no quarter)* It's generally warm in August, isn't it?

RALPH. Well—yes, of course, I was just thinking— well, of course September is cooler—that is—generally—

PATRICK. Do you take a lot of interest in the weather, Mr. Penrose?

MAGGIE. Ralph is interested in lots of things, aren't you, Ralph?

RITA. Are you interested in weather, Mr. Penrose?

ROSALIE. Silly! He's just embarrassed. Papa's trying to get his goat.

MAGGIE. Rosalie, hush!

PATRICK. Not at all, Rosalie. I'm not interested in Mr. Penrose's goat. *(To RALPH, amused)* I haven't got your goat, have I, Mr. Penrose?

RALPH. Aha! Hardly!

(The room lapses into uncomfortable silence. MAG-GIE looks hard at RALPH. He looks at her. She mouths "Say something.")

Ah—speaking of goats, Mr. Flannigan—reminds me of a little story you might like.

(MAGGIE gives a tiny nod of approval at this sally.)

It—it seems there was this travelling salesman who came to a farmhouse—

PATRICK. Young man!

RALPH. Oh, it's not one of those stories, sir! No, no. As I say, there was this travelling salesman who came to a farmhouse, where there was a goat thethered outside. It was a—what-do-you-call-it—a—male—a Billy goat with long whiskers.

ROSALIE. Like Papa's?

RALPH. Yes. Ah—no! No, no of course not. It was a beard more. *(Indicates a long beard with hand)* Yes. Well, anyway, so the goat said, "What's your line, Mister?"

ROSALIE. The goat *talked?*

RALPH. Ah—yes. For the purposes of the story.

ROSALIE. Oh.

RALPH. Ah—so. *(Looks bewildered)* Now where was I?

FINNEGAN. *(Opening his curtains)* The goat said.

RALPH. Oh—yes. So the goat said— *(Pause, realizing that* FINNEGAN *spoke from the curtain)* Does he *live* in there?

MAGGIE. He's staying with us for a few days and we have no guest room. Please go on, Ralph.

RALPH. Oh. Well, so the goat said, "What's your line, Mister?" And the salesman said, "I travel in brushes." So the goat said—

ROSALIE. What does that mean, Mr. Penrose—travel in brushes?

PATRICK. It's a salesman's expression, Rosalie. It means he sells brushes on the road. Continue, Mr. Penrose.

RALPH. Well, so the goat said, "I'm a salesman, too. I'll bet you can't—"

ROSALIE. How can a goat be a salesman?

MAGGIE. Shhh! Rosalie! Stop interrupting all the time.

PATRICK. Your sister has a curious mind, Maggie. Let us do nothing to discourage it. *(To* ROSALIE*)* Again it's for the purposes of the story, Rosalie. It's a whimsical story. Go on, Mr. Penrose.

RALPH. Ah—thank you. Well—let's see—where was I?

FINNEGAN. *(At curtains)* The goat said.

RALPH. Oh—yes. *(Louder so* FINNEGAN *can hear)* Thank you! *(To* OTHERS *in former tone)* The goat said, "I'm a salesman, too, but I'll bet you can't guess what I travel in! I'll give you some of my good goat's milk if you guess." Guess what line the goat was in that is. So the salesman said, "That's easy. If you travel in anything you travel in milk." "Nope," said the goat, I travel in tea. Goat—tea!"

> (FINNEGAN *sticks his head through curtains and looks at* RALPH *in disgust. Closes curtains. After a moment* FINNEGAN'S *arm reaches out, grabs whisky bottle and retires it behind curtains.)*

That's odd. When I first heard the story I thought it was funnier.

MAGGIE. Is that the end—?

ROSALIE. Billy goats don't give milk, do they, Papa?

PATRICK. A well taken point, Rosalie. I believe they do not.

    (ROSALIE *crosses, sits footstool.)*

Tell me, young man—you're connected with the gas company, are you not?

RALPH. Ah—yes, sir, I am.

MAGGIE. Papa, must you start in on that now?

PATRICK. We can't talk about goats all afternoon, Maggie.

FINNEGAN. *(Comes out of alcove)* Patrick—

PATRICK. Oh, Finnegan. Have you met Mr. Penrose?

FINNEGAN. *(Left of* RALPH*)* Yes, we've met. I just wanted to tell you that I dropped in on poor Big Jim O'Malley this morning.

PATRICK. *(Blank)* Big Jim who?

FINNEGAN. *(Playing it off* RALPH*)* O'Malley. Don't tell me you've forgotten? The fellow you knocked out last week. A little disagreement over politics. O'Malley has a broken nose and two broken ribs, it seems. *(To* PATRICK*)* I just thought you'd like to know that Jim's doing nicely at the hospital, and he asked me to tell you that he bears you no grudge.

ROSALIE. You didn't tell us you had a fight, Papa?

PATRICK. Well, I—I forgot about it, I guess.

FINNEGAN. There's your father for you— *(For* RALPH'*s uneasy benefit)* Quick to anger and quick to forget. *(He gives* RALPH *a meaningful stare, then exits back into cubicle.)*

MAGGIE. *(Herself nervous, anxious to dispel the effect of* FINNEGAN'*s story on the uneasy* RALPH*)* I assure you, Ralph, Papa is not as dangerous as he sounds.

RALPH. Ha! Oh, I'm sure he—he isn't.

MAGGIE. Why you haven't fought with anyone in years, Papa, have you?

PATRICK. Not until last week apparently.

RITA. Are you going to fight Mr. Penrose, Papa?

PATRICK. No, Rita—

RITA. Oh!

PATRICK. —at least I don't think so. *(To* RALPH*)* The two young ones are convinced that you and I will come to blows this afternoon, Mr. Penroose.

RALPH. *(Nervously)* Aha—

PATRICK. They know I hold some rather strong views about your company.

RALPH. Aha—I'm sure—

PATRICK. *(Crosses down Right. Takes philosophic tone)* Young man, I'd like to ask you a question. What spiritual satisfaction do you get out of gas?

RALPH. Spiritual—?

PATRICK. *(Crosses to landing)* Yes! Take me. I'm a builder. When I build a house that is something which gives me satisfaction as well as a living. Now what satisfaction do you find in gas?

RALPH. Oh—well— *(He looks thoughtfully stumped.)*

PATRICK. I see you have difficulty answering. *(To above table)* As well you might! Because you're part of a corrupt conspiracy to defraud the public of light!

RALPH. Well—

PATRICK. *(More and more oratorical as he warms to attack)* There you sit, like a great complacent leech. Sapping the life blood of progress. Blocking the future. And why?

MAGGIE. Papa, you're not addressing a meeting and Ralph is not the whole gas company.

PATRICK. Well, what is he then? *(To* RALPH*)* What *is* your position down there?

RALPH. Well, my family made me Vice President.

PATRICK. There! And what could be worse. *(To* RALPH*)* Everytime I'm forced to build a new house with your medieval gas pipes in my walls I— *(He crosses Right.)*

RALPH. Mr. Flannigan! I *believe* in electricity.

PATRICK. *(Wind taken out of his sails)* What—?

RALPH. Yes, sir! I *believe* in electricity.

PATRICK. You do—?

RALPH. *(Rises)* I certainly do. I think electric light means progress and by George—well—I *believe in progress!* Why, only yesterday I wrote a *memo* to that effect.

PATRICK. Did you now? *(Crosses in.)*

RALPH. I certainly did. I said—*I* say let the lighting fixtures go and push the gas stove instead!

PATRICK. *(Enthusiastic)* Exactly. The gas stove. You're right! As I said in my letter to the paper—

RALPH. I read that letter. And I agree with it one hundred percent. I even attached it to my *memo*.

PATRICK. *Did* you now? Well—! And what did they say to all this?

RALPH. Well, you see, sir, nobody listens to me down there.

PATRICK. Then what are you doing down there in the first place? A boy with your vision. Your intelligence.

RALPH. Well—a man has to do *something*.

PATRICK. Something as useless and retrogressive as that? Do you need blood money?

RALPH. Well—well, you see my parents—kind of shoved me into gas. They insisted and—

PATRICK. *(Innocently trapping himself)* And who are they to insist? Parents be damned! It's your life, isn't it? Live it by yourself. No sane person cuts his life to another's will.

MAGGIE. *(Rises)* You're absolutely right, Papa! *To* OTHERS) Papa's absolutely right!

MARY. Absolutely.

RITA *and* ROSALIE. Yes, absolutely.

PATRICK. Absolutely. I'd like to hear that you're *out* of that gas house by tomorrow! *(Sits chair Right)* Stand up to your family!

MAGGIE. *(Seated. In high spirits, eager)* Ralph. I think the proper moment has come for you to speak up.

PATRICK. I wouldn't wait another minute, son.

RALPH. Oh you mean—well she means—you mean *now?*

MAGGIE. Yes, Ralph.

PATRICK. What's this—what are you talking about?

MAGGIE. Ralph will explain, Papa. *(To* RALPH) Ralph.

RALPH. *(Rises)* Ah—yes. Well, sir— *(Above Morris chair)* Sir, Mr. Flannigan, I know this may seem quite abrupt—in fact it *is* abrupt but—well, you see, sir, we're in an awful hurry and—that is—no! I don't mean that. What I mean is—well, as you know I came here today— *(Hesitates)* Oh, but wait—you didn't know that, did you—?

PATRICK. I know you came here today. Kindly proceed from there.

RALPH. Ah—yes. Well, Maggie and I—we'd rather like to—we were wondering if—perhaps I should put it more definitely. Ah—we were definitely—ah—wondering if— if we could get married—if that's all right with you, sir—?

PATRICK. *(Rises; crosses to* MARY)

(RALPH *sits Left as he rises.)*

I suspected something like this. *(Pause. Then in a loud voice that makes* RALPH *jump) Mary!*

MARY. Y-yes, Papa?

PATRICK. I recently gave you a message to be transmitted to your sister. Did you transmit it?

MARY. You mean about—about nobody getting married for just ages yet, Papa. Yes, I did.

PATRICK. There was more to the message than that. Among other things I suggested that your sister forget all about this nonsense.

MARY. I—I *think* I mentioned that—

PATRICK. Very well. My suggestion apparently went by the board. Therefore any embarrassment incurred at this moment is not of my choosing. *(To* RALPH) Young man, your answer is a categorical *no!*

RALPH. Oh—

ROSALIE. What's categorical mean, Papa?

PATRICK. It means *no! (To above table)* Are you aware, sir, that my daughter has been officially accepted at Vassar College?

MAGGIE. *(Rises)* Papa, you said no sane person cuts his life to another's will. Well, it's your will for me to go to college. But I want to marry Ralph. And by your own advice—that's what I *should* do!

PATRICK. Well you won't while I'm conscious, young lady. You're under age and require my consent.

MAGGIE. *(Short pause, then firmly)* Is that your last word, Papa?

PATRICK. My last. And the last on this subject I trust. *(Crosses Right.)*

MAGGIE. Very well. Sisters, I wish to put the question of my marriage before the family council.

(GIRLS *collect chairs, gavel, etc.; prepare for meeting.*)

PATRICK. What—? Are you out of your mind? Since when does the family council decide about marriages?

MAGGIE. Well, it never has before, Papa, because none of us has ever been proposed to before. It's your turn to be chairman, isn't it, Rosalie.

ROSALIE. I'm Madam Chairman.

PATRICK. Now wait a minute. I'm not ready for the meeting right now. And no meeting's valid unless I participate.

MAGGIE. Are you ill, Papa?

PATRICK. Ill? Of course not.

MAGGIE. Section three, paragraph two of the by-laws states that no member may refuse to attend a meeting except by reason of illness.

MARY. Or unless he's been properly excused by the other members.

ROSALIE. All in favor of excusing Papa say "aye."

PATRICK. Aye.

ROSALIE. Opposed?

FOUR SISTERS. Nay!

PATRICK. *(Marytyr's tone—crossing in)* Oh, so you've got them all lined up against me, have you? *(To MAG-GIE)* You've got the whole council lined up against your poor old father.

MAGGIE. If you really respect it please sit down so we can begin.

PATRICK. I will not sit down! I'll have nothing to do with it! *(Crosses Right.)*

MAGGIE. *(Crosses down)* Papa, the very first time a really serious question is to be brought before the council you balk and run out on it! What is the council for then? Just to decide who will wash dishes? Or has it some *meaning!* If you *do* refuse me this meeting, I for one will never believe in anything you say again.

PATRICK. *(Crosses around table; looks at her serious, defiant young face for a moment in silence. Then he shrugs angrily)* All right, all right—start the meeting. But I warn you—

ROSALIE. *(Pounding gavel)* Please sit down, everybody. Meeting come to order.

(PATRICK hits RALPH to get him out of chair. RALPH rises and sits chaise. PATRICK takes chair.)

RALPH. *(Sincere enthusiasm)* By George, sir, this is really a remarkable way to run a family. I don't believe I've ever seen anything like this before.

PATRICK. I'm not sure I have either! *(To GIRLS)* Now I warn you girls. This family council is not supposed to be a conspiratorial body. If I find—

MAGGIE. Are you suggesting that if all your daughters *dare* to disagree with you—that is a conspiracy?

PATRICK. I'm not suggesting, I'm saying *outright* that some sort of bribery has been going on around here.

MAGGIE. I'm sure it has, Papa—often. Rosalie, didn't Papa bribe you to vote for Mr. Finnegan the other day?

ROSALIE. Papa just promised me a whole box of chocolates, that's all.

PATRICK. *(Righteous)* They were not a bribe. The child likes chocolates so I gave her some.

ROSALIE. You didn't give them to me yet, Papa.

PATRICK. Shhh! Is it bribery when a father gives to his child?

ROSALIE. *(To RITA)* But he didn't give them to me yet!

PATRICK. Quiet! It was simply a gift, Maggie. If the child later happened to vote my way it was purely co-incidental.

MAGGIE. I'm glad to hear you say that, Papa. Madam Chairman, may I state my reason for calling this meeting?

ROSALIE. Yes, Maggie. Go ahead.

MAGGIE. *(Rises)* It's very simple. I want to marry Mr. Penrose. I'm not of legal age yet so I need Papa's consent. I therefore move that the family council *order* Papa to give his consent.

MARY. Second the motion.

PATRICK. *(On his feet again)* I object!

ROSALIE. The chair has not recognized you yet, Papa.

PATRICK. Well, you'd better recognize me! I'm your father!

MAGGIE. *(Rises)* Madam Chairman, that constitutes a threat against the person of the chair.

PATRICK. Nonsense. *How* did I threaten her?

ROSALIE. You said you're my father.

PATRICK. That does *not* necessarily constitute a threat.

ROSALIE. Pay the fine.

(MARY *holds out the fine box.)*

PATRICK. Oh, all right. There. To keep you quiet. *(He puts a coin in the box)* But I just wanted to say— *(Sits.)*

ROSALIE. *(Pounds gavel)* Are you finished, Maggie?

MAGGIE. Yes, Madam Chairman. *(Sits.)*

ROSALIE. It has been moved and seconded that Papa allow Maggie to get married. All those in favor—

PATRICK. *(Seated)* Madam Chairman, when are you going to throw the floor open for discussion of this unspeakable motion?

ROSALIE. Yes, Papa. The floor is open for discussion.

(PATRICK *rises.)*

Papa—?

PATRICK. *(Crosses above chair)* Thank you. It is my

deep conviction that marriage is no proper matter for this family council to decide. I say—

MAGGIE. Papa's own preamble clearly states that all important matters must be brought before the family council!

PATRICK. How about keeping some other people in order around here, Madam Chairman?

ROSALIE. You're out of order, Maggie. *(Taps.)*

PATRICK. Thank you, Madam Chairman— I therefore move that this meeting be adjourned before you all do something you'll be sorry for later!

MAGGIE. That's another threat.

MARY. Pay the fine, Papa.

PATRICK. *(Feels in pocket, finds only a quarter)* I have no more change. *(He puts the quarter in the box)* There's two bits. That will cover my next four threats!

MAGGIE. Rosalie, if there's no further discussion we can put my motion to the vote now.

PATRICK. There *is* further discussion. And I still have the floor.

ROSALIE. Yes, Papa, you still have the floor. *(As he hesitates)* What do you want to say?

PATRICK. *(Talking on as he tries to think of a way out)* Well now according to Paragraph Four of the by-laws which clearly states— *(By now he has paced over to the cubicle, which gives him an idea. He turns and his tone is firm)* Before this motion is put to the vote I think all members of the family council should be present.

RITA. We are, Papa—

PATRICK. Are we indeed? I don't see the new member of our family here.

RITA. Who—?

PATRICK. Mr. Leonard Finnegan!

MAGGIE. Mr. Finnegan! *(Rises)* Oh, Madam Chairman. Please remind Papa that this family council consists of our family. Not Papa's friends and just anybody who will vote Papa's way!

PATRICK. It's obvious that Finnegan is entitled to membership here. He is living under our roof and eating at our table.

MAGGIE. Madam Chairman, Papa is trying to railroad Mr. Finnegan into this because he'll bring Papa a lot of extra votes. And there is absolutely nothing in the constitution—

PATRICK. Exactly. Absolutely nothing that defines the *membership* of the council. You choose to assume it refers only to us, but I say it refers to all living under my roof. And I wrote it. I ought to know. *(Crosses to bar decisively.)*

MAGGIE. *(After whispering with* GIRLS*)* Very well. Madam Chairman, I move this meeting be adjourned—

PATRICK. Second the motion.

MAGGIE. I haven't finished, sir—for *five minutes* at which time the family council will reconvene for further deliberations.

PATRICK. *(Crosses to her)* What for? There are no further deliberations to deliberate. Either you accept Finnegan or—

ROSALIE. *(Gavel)* You're out of order, Papa.

(He quiets down.)

It has been moved and seconded that this meeting adjourn for five minutes and then meet again. All in favor say "aye."

THE GIRLS. Aye!

ROSALIE. Opposed?

PATRICK. Nay! *(Gives up)* Aye then. And run along. Five minutes is five minutes.

(MAGGIE, MARY *exit upstairs.*)

ROSALIE. *(Rises; crosses to* RALPH*)* Gee, Mr. Penrose, that's just time to drive us around the block!

RITA. *(Crosses to* RALPH*)* Yes, Ralphie—will you?

RALPH. Well, I—

ROSALIE. Don't you think Mr. Penrose should, Papa?

PATRICK. *(Wanting them out of the way)* Yes, young man, that's a fine idea. Very nice of you.

ROSALIE. Oh good! Come on, Mr. Penrose. *(She takes him by the hand and starts pulling.)*

RITA. *(Also pulling)* Can I sit up in front, Mr. Penrose?

RALPH. *(As he is being pulled to front door)* Mr. Flannigan, I want to say this, sir. In all my life I've never seen such a brilliant method of running a family— it's so fair—so honest— Yes, I'm coming!

(He and LITTLE GIRLS *go out.)*

PATRICK. *(Crosses to Right, then to alcove)* Finnegan— Finnegan!

*(*FINNEGAN *emerges in a state of intoxication.)*
*(*PATRICK *shakes him)* Pull yourself together. *(He takes* FINNEGAN *to chaise.* PATRICK *sits Morris chair.* PATRICK *reaches to table for pencil and paper. As he does,* FINNEGAN *almost falls over on chaise)* Finnegan, did you hear what's been going on in this room?

FINNEGAN. Discretion induced me to snooze. Or was it that story about a goat?

PATRICK. You heard nothing then?

FINNEGAN. Well, I did seem to hear something about Maggie getting married if the council votes in her favor.

PATRICK. You must join the family council and vote— need I say which way?

FINNEGAN. *(Rises)* Now, Patrick—I'm a man of peace. I'd rather not get entangled.

PATRICK. *(Rises)* Finnegan, would you pass by a man in distress? This is my daughter! She's drowning in a— in a bog of romance. Would you have it on your conscience that you did not give me a helping hand?

FINNEGAN. Well—if you put it that way—

PATRICK. You're a gentleman. Thank you. *(Seats* FINNEGAN. *Rises; crosses to table. Gets pad and pencil)* Finnegan, how old are you?

FINNEGAN. I'm forty-one.

PATRICK. Shhh! Forty'one. No, no. You're older than that.

FINNEGAN. What—?

PATRICK. You're— *(Slight pause)* —forty-five.

FINNEGAN. Forty-five!

PATRICK. Sssh!

FINNEGAN. Why?

PATRICK. *(Crosses to chair Left)* Because my bones tell me there's something going on around here—what I don't know. But I'm in an extraordinary situation here and—

FINNEGAN. I'm the one in—

(PATRICK *shushes him.*)

(He continues in a lower voice) I'm the one in the extraordinary situation. I don't think I look forty-five. Besides, my age is a matter of record.

PATRICK. There'll be no checking of records here.

(At this moment MAGGIE *appears on the stairs.)*

Ahem! As I was saying, Finnegan—

(MAGGIE *comes downstairs full of purpose. We hear the CAR stopping outside.)*

—there are things going on in this world today that are almost incredible. Take the flying machine. *(After* MAGGIE *goes out front door)* —Are you with me, Finnegan?

FINNEGAN. All right, Patrick. As long as it's you.

(MAGGIE *re-enters, followed by* RITA *and* ROSALIE *and* RALPH. MARY *comes from upstairs. They take their places.)*

PATRICK. Did you have a nice ride?

RITA. Hum? Oh, yes, Papa. Very nice indeed, thank you.

PATRICK. *(To* RALPH) Sit down, young man.

ROSALIE. *(Pounds gavel briefly)* The meeting will come to order.

MAGGIE. Madam Chairman, I suggest we dispense with the reading of minutes and proceed directly to unfinished business.

ROSALIE. Are there any objections?

(None.)

In that case, Maggie, do you wish to speak?

MAGGIE. Yes, Madam Chairman. *(Rises. To* PATRICK) Papa, you have suggested that Mr. Finnegan join the family council. Am I correct in stating that you feel he is eligible because he sleeps under our roof and eats at our table?

PATRICK. That's right.

MAGGIE. Very well, Papa. On that basis, we will accept Mr. Finnegan—if you accept Mrs. Gallup.

PATRICK. (PATRICK *is electrified. He jumps up and crosses to* FINNEGAN) You see what I mean! *(To* MAGGIE—*stalling)* She's a prejudiced woman.

MAGGIE. Mr. Finnegan is a prejudiced man!

PATRICK. Finnegan—come here.

(FINNEGAN *rises. They confer.*)

(PATRICK *seems reassured)* All right. Bring on Mrs. Gallup.

(FINNEGAN *sits.* PATRICK *sits Morris chair.*)

RITA. *(Running Left and calling)* Mrs. Gallup.

MRS. GALLUP. *(Off)* Yes, Rita.

(RITA *returns to her seat.*)

MAGGIE. And Papa, do you solemnly swear by your sacred word of honor to abide by the decision of the council as so constituted?

PATRICK. *(Rises—hand up)* I do. Do you swear the same and with equal solemnity?

MAGGIE. *(Hand up)* I do.

PATRICK. *(He sits)* Very well then. Now maybe we'll settle this matter for good.

MRS. GALLUP. *(Entering)* Yes, Mr. Flannigan!

PATRICK. Oh, Mrs. Gallup, do you know Mr. Penrose?

MRS. GALLUP. Oh, how do you do, Mr. Penrose?

RALPH. *(Sits)* How do you do?

PATRICK. *(Indicating chaise)* Sit down, Mrs. Gallup.

(She sits. FINNEGAN *moves away.)*

Madam Secretary, will you please state the motion before the board?

MARY. *(Rises)* This is a meeting of the family council and you've both been invited to participate with us. The issue before us is whether Maggie should be allowed to marry that young man. The council will decide and you will vote along with us. Are there any questions?

MRS. GALLUP. I must warn you, Mr. Flannigan, that if you call on me to vote I—

PATRICK. I assume you will vote your convictions, Mam. Oh, first let me remind you that in this family council each person casts as many votes as his or her age. *(He looks at her with quiet amusement.)*

MRS. GALLUP. Oh dear—I—I'd forgotten that—

PATRICK. I trust you have no objection to revealing the number of your votes, Mam?

MRS. GALLUP. But couldn't we just vote normally— one vote each—?

PATRICK. Unfortunately, it is against the rules, Mam.

MRS. GALLUP. *(Hesitates)* Well—all right—

MAGGIE. *(Rising)* It has been moved and seconded that the family council order Papa to give his immediate legal consent to my marriage with Mr. Penrose.

ROSALIE. *(Gavel)* Now we will vote in the usual way. You keep the record, Madam Secretary. I start with me. I cast ten votes—yes! Rita?

(FINNEGAN *rises; crosses above* PATRICK.)

RITA. Seven votes—yes.

ROSALIE. Mary?

MARY. Sixteen votes—yes.

ROSALIE. Maggie?

MAGGIE. Seventeen votes—yes.

ROSALIE. Mrs. Gallup?

MRS. GALLUP. I vote *for* marriage—forty votes.

ROSALIE. Papa?

(PATRICK *is so engrossed in figuring on a pad that he*

does not respond at once.)
Papa!

PATRICK. Oh! Forty-five votes—*no!*

ROSALIE. Mr. Finnegan?

FINNEGAN. *(Looks at pad)* Forty-six votes—no. *(He walks away sourly.)*

MAGGIE. Forty-six— Oh Mr. Finnegan!

MARY. Oh, Mr. Finnegan!

MRS. GALLUP. Why, Mr. Finnegan, I'd never dream you were that old!

FINNEGAN. *(Sits chaise)* I'm often told my age sits well on me, Mam.

PATRICK. What is your count, Madam Secretary?

MARY. *(Rising—with pencil and paper)* Ninety votes in favor. Ninety-one against.

PATRICK. Well, that makes it official.

(MARY *rises and starts to go upstairs.)*

MAGGIE. This vote is not official yet.

PATRICK. Where are you going, Mary?

MARY. I have to go upstairs to get something. *(To* ROSALIE) Don't close the voting till I get back. *(She runs off upstairs.)*

MAGGIE. Papa, you know very well that Mr. Finnegan is younger than you are!

PATRICK. What? He most certainly is not.

MAGGIE. Papa, you've always said that he is.

PATRICK. When have I ever said such a thing?

MAGGIE. Why Papa, you've always told the story that when you were children once you gave Finnegan his bottle in the crib—and he was only six months old. How could you have done that if he's older than you are?

PATRICK. *(Embarrassed)* Well—I was a very big baby —that was the point of the story.

MAGGIE. But, Papa, you'd have to have been *not* born *yet!*

PATRICK. Well, maybe Finnegan fed me then. That was it, wasn't it, Finnegan?

FINNEGAN. It must have been me that gave you the bottle!

PATRICK. Yes!

ROSALIE. But Papa you always said—

(MAGGIE *crosses up Center.*)

PATRICK. *(Rises)* How dare you question the age of your elders. No one questioned your ages.
(They are all silenced.)
(He turns to RALPH*)* You see, there you are, young man. *(Crosses below to Right)* This is why women have to be trained. They're irrational by temperament. They don't want justice—they want their own way.
(MARY *starts down steps.*)
Now you as a man, can accept a decision like this even if it goes against you.

RALPH. *(Rises)* Well—yes, sir—it would be dishonorable not to.

(MARY *returns to table, carrying a book.* FINNEGAN *crosses to her. She slides into place and whispers to* ROSALIE.)

ROSALIE. Before making this vote a matter of record, I would like to take the floor.

PATRICK. *(Crosses to up Center)* What for?

ROSALIE. *(Crosses to* MRS. GALLUP*)* Mrs. Gallup, I have here a book. It is the Holy Bible. Would you lay your hand on it and solemnly swear you have only forty votes?

PATRICK. *(Crosses to Left Center on the run)* No, she will not! And I'm shocked you should ask such a thing! How dare you question this good woman's votes? If she had more votes wouldn't she say so?

ROSALIE. That's what we want to find out, Papa.

PATRICK. *(Crosses Center)* Can I believe my ears. *(To* FINNEGAN*)* Isn't this a shock to you, Finnegan.

FINNEGAN. It certainly is a shock to me.

MAGGIE. Papa, you're out of order.

MARY. Right, Maggie.

RITA. Yes, Papa.

PATRICK. This whole meeting is out of order. This unspeakable attack on Mrs. Gallup's privacy is out of order.

ROSALIE. Papa. It's you that's out of order. Now sit down, please. I don't want to fine you again. *(She pounds gavel, then stands looking at* PATRICK *commandingly.)*

(They ALL *sit.)*

PATRICK. They're using the Holy Scriptures to further their own ends, Finnegan.

FINNEGAN. *(Exiting into alcove)* I can't stand it.

ROSALIE. Now—where were we? Oh, yes. Well, Mrs. Gallup, will you swear on the bible that you have only forty votes?

(MRS. GALLUP *has been looking around rather frantically during all the foregoing. Now she slowly drops into tears, taking out her handkerchief. She rises and exits upstairs.)*

(ROSALIE *follows her to up Center)* Oh—please, Mrs. Gallup—don't cry—

PATRICK. Now look what you've done! Aren't you ashamed.

ROSALIE. *(Right of table)* Papa, Mrs. Gallup is crying because she's got more votes.

PATRICK. How do you know?

ROSALIE. That is Mrs. Gallup's family bible. The date of her birth is recorded in it.

MARY. *(Opens the bible. Rises)* She was born in eighteen sixty-seven. That makes her forty-five. She has five whole extra votes she didn't say anything about.

PATRICK. What— Let me see that bible! *(He grabs it from* ROSALIE. *He sits chaise.)*

MARY. Maggie, you've won. You've won. Ninety-five for you and only ninety-one for Papa. Let's go and tell Mrs. Gallup the exciting news.

(CHILDREN *exit upstairs shouting "We've won, Mrs.
    Gallup, we've won!"*)

MAGGIE. Ralph, we've won. *(Kneels beside her father)*
I think we should set a date for the wedding now, Papa.

RALPH. *(Crosses to Left Center)* By George, sir. This
is simply immense.

PATRICK. *(Crosses down Right)* Nonsense! I'll not be
bound by this Tammany Hall maneuvering.

RALPH. But sir, you said we men know how to accept a
civilized decision. *(Crosses to* PATRICK.)

PATRICK. So you consider it civilized to suggest the
ruin of my daughter?

RALPH. Sir, I don't want to ruin her. I just want to
marry her. I love her!

PATRICK. *(Backs* RALPH *across to down Left Center)*
Love, you say! And is it in the name of love that you'd
strangle this innocent creature's growth? Cut off her
culture, trample her intelligence, and leave her a trem-
bling mass of ignorance for the rest of her days?

RALPH. Good Lord—no, sir— But—

PATRICK. Aren't you ashamed of yourself?

MAGGIE. *(Between them)* How dare you speak to Ralph
in such a way. *I* choose my husband. And *I* choose when
to marry him!

PATRICK. Not while you're seventeen, young lady!

MAGGIE. I may be seventeen in age, but I'm not seventeen in my heart—and I know what I want!

PATRICK. You know nothing of what you want! *(To*
RALPH) You! You're the cause of all this! She was a
sane, sensible girl—then you came along like the snake
after Eve, weaving and twisting your coils around her,
spilling poison in her ear, tempting her with the evil apple
of ignorance! Get out! *(He has driven* RALPH *out the
kitchen door, turns his back)* Well—

RALPH. *(Returning)* But sir! The apple was knowledge.

PATRICK. *Silence!* Get out.

    (RALPH *goes.*)

(PATRICK *looks at the defiant, angry* MAGGIE *for a*

moment. He crosses to Left of table) I'm sorry I had to do that. But what must be done must be done.

MAGGIE. *(Low voice—deeply hurt, crosses to stairs)* Yes, Papa, I think you will be sorry you did that.

PATRICK. *(To her)* Maggie you'll not play hob with the one most important thing—your education.

MAGGIE. The one most important thing to you, perhaps. But you've just played hob with the most important thing to me.

PATRICK. You'll take the best life has to offer, even if I must force you to accept it.

(As she talks the three younger GIRLS *come out on the stair landing to watch her and as she finishes her speech, they raise a cheer.)*

MAGGIE. I intend to. A nice decent boy came to call on me. A boy who loves me and wants to marry me—and my big, broad-minded liberal talking father insulted him and humiliated me. I won the right to be married here this afternoon and you took it away from me. You always said it yourself. The Flannigans were never made for tyranny. All right. You have asked for it. This means *war!* (MAGGIE *runs off up stairs.)*

CURTAIN

ACT THREE

AT RISE: *The stage is empty. From the kitchen come the sounds of CLINKING and CLATTER. RITA and ROSALIE come downstairs. ROSALIE has an alarm clock, RITA a balloon. Both creep over to the kitchen door and listen.*

ROSALIE. Papa's trying to cook his own breakfast. *(They giggle.)*
Where shall we put this? *(Indicating alarm clock.)*
    RITA. There's a good place? *(Indicating shelf off stairway.)*
    ROSALIE. Where? Oh, wonderful! *(She sets the clock.)*
    RITA. *(Hides balloon behind Morris chair. Then ROSALIE indicates to RITA that she should go upstairs and she herself goes out the front door. Half way up RITA says)*
Ready—
    MARY. *(Off)* Ready!

(From upstairs comes a crash and RITA runs up. PATRICK and FINNEGAN dash in from kitchen. PATRICK is wearing one of MRS. GALLUP'S aprons.)

PATRICK. What was that!

(Another CRASH is heard.)

FINNEGAN. This *is* war!
    PATRICK. *(Crosses to foot of stairs)* Now what's going on up there? I'll not have this house a shambles— What was that noise?

(The alarm clock goes off.)
(PATRICK *answers phone, then realizes his mistake)* Where
is it   Where is it? Do you see it, Finnegan?
FINNEGAN. No, but I definitely hear it.

(BOTH MEN *look around for source of bell.)*

PATRICK. Ah! Here it is. *(He shuts it off.)*
    (The DOORBELL rings.)
All right! All right! I'm coming. *(Tearing off his apron
he crosses to the door.)*
FINNEGAN. I smell something burning. *(He exits into
the kitchen.)*
PATRICK. *(Opens the door)*
    (Some brooms fall in.)
Rita! Rosalie! I might have known!
FINNEGAN. *(Enters)* Patrick, your eggs are burning.
PATRICK. Well, don't just stand there, do something!
(Picking up apron and putting it on.)
FINNEGAN. Oh!

(BOTH *exit to the kitchen.* ROSALIE *comes in front door.*
    RITA *comes downstairs.)*

ROSALIE. They're in the kitchen. Is it ready?
RITA. Yes. *(She hands* ROSALIE *string for Victrola.)*

(ROSALIE *attaches it to starter of phonograph. The other
    end of the string leads off up the stairs. The* GIRLS
    exit upstairs. PATRICK *and* FINNEGAN *re-enter.* PAT-
    RICK *is carrying a cup of coffee and* FINNEGAN *a
    beer.)*

PATRICK. *(Sits Morris chair)* I'm afraid the manu-
facture of breakfast is not my forte, Finnegan.
FINNEGAN. I'm just a consumer myself. *(Sits Left of
table.)*
PATRICK. Sure you won't try some of my coffee?
FINNEGAN. Thank you, no. I have found after many

years that the barley is the only thing I can keep down before the noon whistle blows. Well, here's how—

(From stairs ROSALIE *blows a pea shooter which hits* FINNEGAN *in the neck.* FINNEGAN *jumps.)*

PATRICK. Ignore it!
FINNEGAN. *(Outraged)* Ignore it!

(Victrola starts as GIRLS *yank string.* PATRICK *rises in a rage and turns off Victrola. Then he pulls the string attached to it. A pail and cowbells come tumbling down the stairs. They take him by surprise.)*

FINNEGAN. Ignore it!
PATRICK. *(Wearily discarding pail and cowbells)* I made a mistake yesterday. I should never have taken the full brunt of their attack on myself.
FINNEGAN. What else could you do?
PATRICK. *(Crosses to sit)* A ha, what else indeed. What does a head of state do when his domain is threatened by the invasion of a foreign power? He seeks an alliance. A strategic alliance. You may have noticed that I left the house last night? I went to see the Penroses.
FINNEGAN. A ha!
PATRICK. From now on the halter will be put around that young man's neck right where it should be—in his own house. I've cut off the boy supply at the source. Strategy, Finnegan, strategy. Incidentally, we discussed the gas company problems and I found him surprisingly amenable. Fact is, I'm awaiting momentarily a change in the gas company policy.
FINNEGAN. *(Looks at* PATRICK, *then at the paper)* Funny you should say that. *(Reads)* "No Change in Gas Company Policy."
PATRICK. What?
FINNEGAN. "Mr. Augustus W. Penrose announced late last night that—"

PATRICK. *(Taking paper)* Let me see that. (PATRICK *reads the paper.)*

FINNEGAN. *(Picks up a letter and examines it)* Got a registered letter from my "ex" this morning. I couldn't face it on an empty stomach but now that I've had something to sustain me— *(He opens the letter, reads, his face clouding)* Ah dear—that woman, that woman. If I went to my grave I do believe she'd follow me in to claw me.

PATRICK. What's the matter now?

FINNEGAN. It seems the Harpie has found out that I quit my job to escape her alimony. And that I am malingering, so Her Highness stipulates that I have five days in which to pay up back alimony "or else you are to be incarcerated again."

PATRICK. What! Why that beast of prey! Let me see the letter!

(FINNEGAN *passes it to him.)*

(PATRICK *reads it quickly)* This is something new. "If you will make a final setlement of five hundred dollars, we will waive all past and future claims of alimony." Why, Finnegan, this is wonderful—you'll be free of her at last.

FINNEGAN. A consumation devoutly to be wished. Can you lend me five hundred dollars?

PATRICK. No, I'm sorry I can't. Not with four girls and all my expenses.

FINNEGAN. There you have it.

PATRICK. Now wait a minute. The trouble with you is, Finnegan, you always give up too easily. We have to think—use our gray matter.

FINNEGAN. It's a knotty problem for a mere man.

PATRICK. Do you know *anyone* who could lend you the money?

FINNEGAN. Yes. J. P. Morgan. But he hasn't dropped into the pool room of late.

PATRICK. The problem is essentially simple. We have only to bring you and five hundred dollars together.

FINNEGAN. That would be a charming meeting.

PATRICK. There must be a way—

(BOTH MEN *think*. MRS. GALLUP *appears at the top of the stairs, taking off her glasses as she sees them. She is dressed to go out, with her hat on. She is looking much more presentable than heretofore. She is wearing a new dress, more gay than her usual attire. She is conscious of the change in herself and wonders if the men will notice it.*)

MRS. GALLUP. Good morning, Mr. Flannigan.

PATRICK. Good morning, Mrs.—

MRS. GALLUP. (*Simpering warmly. Crosses Left above*) Good morning, Mr. Finnegan.

FINNEGAN. A moment please. Something is missing— now don't tell me. (*Studies her a moment*) Ah—no glasses!

MRS. GALLUP. (*Above chaise*) I—I'm afraid I broke them this morning.

FINNEGAN. Was that the sound we heard a few moments ago?

MRS. GALLUP. Hum? Oh—you mean—oh, no. Those girls have been making such a rumpus. I'm afraid they're in quite a mood this morning, Mr. Flannigan. (*At sideboard*) I'm rather glad it's my day off.

PATRICK. (*He indicates her face*) Mrs. Gallup, that's quite a pleasant metamorphosis, without your glasses. I wonder you didn't break them before.

MRS. GALLUP. It's just terrible without them— Well, I think I'll just have a cup of tea before I step out. (*She exits into kitchen.*)

PATRICK. (*Rises; crosses Left*) Extraordinary. This clears up something that has always puzzled me. I can now begin to understand how the late Mr. Gallup blundered into wedlock. Her appearance is really quite—

FINNEGAN. Horrible. Yes. Well, where were we before—

PATRICK. Where we were before, Finnegan, is not where we are now. We were stumped before. Now—I think I have your solution.

FINNEGAN. You have? What?

PATRICK. *(Crosses to* FINNEGAN*)* Strange how life can change an entire situation in the flickering of an eyelid. Before I tell you what I have in mind, let me point out that all life is essentially a compromise, Finnegan. And there are occasions when it is necessary to choose the lesser of two evils. Do you follow me?

FINNEGAN. Not an inch so far, but go on.

PATRICK. *(Crosses to above table)* In order to extricate yourself from great difficulties it is sometimes necessary to leap backwards as it were—from the fire into the frying pan.

FINNEGAN. Go on.

PATRICK. Thinking along these lines, your solution came to me like that. *(Snaps his fingers)* Now please—don't jump out of your chair. You should marry Mrs. Gallup.

FINNEGAN. *(Jumping out of chair)* What!

PATRICK. Now now now—I said *don't* jump out of your chair.

FINNEGAN. When you suddenly stab me with a thought like that!

PATRICK. Calm yourself. *(Sits him down on chaise)* I know this solution comes as a shock but you have not looked your problem squarely in the face!

FINNEGAN. I just did!

PATRICK. And what an improvement. Now I don't expect you to leap into this move, Finnegan—

FINNEGAN. A—men.

PATRICK. Don't think of it as an *ideal* solution—

FINNEGAN. I won't.

PATRICK. Think of it as a wise compromise. And don't forget, Mrs. Gallup has a small but comfortable inheritance from the late Mr. Gallup and she can bail you out! I must get ready for work! *(He goes to foot of stairs.)*

(ROSALIE *appears at top of stairs, sees him and walks off again, nose in air.)*

Yes! I'm coming upstairs. No further reconnaisance will be necessary!

(MRS. GALLUP *re-enters.)*

Ah, Mrs. Gallup, a great improvement without your glasses! *(To* FINNEGAN*)* Well, hop to it, man. No one ever got castor oil down by looking at the bottle. *(He exits upstairs singing.)*

(MRS. GALLUP *sits down Left of table with tea cup.)*

FINNEGAN. Ah, Mrs. Gallup—what a rare moment this is!

MRS. GALLUP. Why, Mr. Finnegan?

FINNEGAN. Why? Because in this crowded house—we are at last alone together!

MRS. GALLUP. *(Twittering)* Oh—Mr. Finnegan!

FINNEGAN. *(Inspecting her as an artist might a bust)* The change in you—I can't get over it!

MRS. GALLUP. *(Delighted)* Am I—really so—different?

FINNEGAN. If I didn't know it was you, I wouldn't know it was you!

(She giggles delightedly.)
Are you familiar with classical reference?

MRS. GALLUP. Why—no—I'm afraid I'm not.

FINNEGAN. Believe me, mam, the head of Medusa was not more lovely!

MRS. GALLUP. *(Blank)* Medusa?

FINNEGAN. A mythological creature. One look at her was enough to do a man in.

MRS. GALLUP. Oh Mr. Finnegan. Now you're flattering me!

FINNEGAN. Oh no I'm not! Ah, how could you have hidden your light behind a bushel so long? I can't get over the change in you. I used to think of you as just another woman. Now I see you have everything a man could want.

MRS. GALLUP. Mr. Finnegan, do you believe in prophesy?

FINNEGAN. Prophesy, mam?

MRS. GALLUP. Yes. Have you ever experienced it personally. Before you left Mrs. Finnegan—did anyone ever prophesy that you would?

FINNEGAN. Yes, mam. I did. Many times.

MRS. GALLUP. Did it come to you almost mystically? Almost as if you heard a voice?

FINNEGAN. It came to me with perfect clarity—whenever I heard her voice.

MRS. GALLUP. Mr. Finnegan—this is just an imaginary situation of course—but what if there were a man who had—had once married the wrong woman and—well—suppose he finally met the right woman—

FINNEGAN. Go on. Go on.

MRS. GALLUP. A woman who would love him and let him do what he likes. Would—would this poor man be so scarred by his experience that they would miss each other—like ships that pass in the night?

FINNEGAN. *(Eying her thoughtfully)* Conceivably they might collide, mam.

MRS. GALLUP. *(Delighted)* Mr. Finnegan, do you think so—!

FINNEGAN. Ahem. Let us explore this—this hypothesis further.

MRS. GALLUP. Oh, yes!

FINNEGAN. Suppose this bruised and beaten man—scarred beyond recognition—

MRS. GALLUP. It wouldn't matter!

FINNEGAN. Suppose this poor, battered canary needed a loan to set him free from his cage—a loan like this— *(He hands her the letter.)*

MRS. GALLUP. *(Takes the letter. At first she holds it away from her, squinting at it)* Oh—is *this* all! Why that's nothing!

FINNEGAN. You mean—this Florence Nightingale would open the cage?

MRS. GALLUP. Why of course! What's money where love is concerned! And then would he—

FINNEGAN. Ah—we'll cross that bridge when we come to it.

MRS. GALLUP. Oh, of course—naturally—

FINNEGAN. But for the moment am I to assume—
(Touching her) that this angel of mercy would find it in
her heart to—ah—to lend him immediate assistance?

MRS. GALLUP. Why, of course, Mr. Finnegan!

FINNEGAN. Well!

MRS. GALLUP. I can go down to the bank right now—
(Getting up) I'll just clear these things away—

FINNEGAN. No, no. Let me do it for you. And I'll tidy
up the kitchen while you're gone.

(MRS. GALLUP *goes out front door.* FINNEGAN *delightedly
takes dishes into kitchen, singing as he goes and
doing a dance step on exit. We hear DISHES crash
to floor.* MARY *appears on top of stairs and watches
till he disappears.*)

MARY. Come on, Maggie. I think the coast is clear.
(MAGGIE *comes hurriedly down, followed by* RITA
and ROSALIE. *There is a suppressed excitement in all
the girls, particularly* MAGGIE.)
Are you really going to do it, Maggie?

MAGGIE. Shhh! Mary, watch this door.
(MARY *goes to kitchen door.*)
Rita! Stay there and watch out for Papa.

MARY. It's so exciting.

MAGGIE. Shh now! *(She goes to telephone, cranks and
listens breathlessly)* One one four—ring one please.

MARY. What if one of his parents—

MAGGIE. Sshhh! *(She listens on phone a moment longer)* Hello, may I speak to Mr. Ralph Penrose, please. Just
say—Miss Flannigan!

MARY. Who answered?

MAGGIE. Shhh! The butler!

MARY. Butler!

ROSALIE. Butler!

RITA. Butler!

MAGGIE. *(On phone)* Hello, Ralph. Yes, darling, it's
me—Maggie. Now I've got to talk quietly because Papa
is still in the house. I've thought it all over and I've made

up my mind. You remember we talked of eloping if Papa
refused us. Well, *now* I'm ready— *(Listens)* What? You
still want to elope, don't you? *(Listens)* Oh— *(Listens)*
Oh— *(Listens)* What!

    (KIDS *move in.*)

(Listens) My father? *(Listens)* Oh—how could he!
(Listens) Why don't you stand up to your family! I
stood up to Papa! *(Listens)* I see. *(Hangs up)* I see.

MARY. *(Crosses Left Center)* What happened? What
did he say?

MAGGIE. *(Above table)* His family's threatening to
disinherit him if he marries me and he doesn't have the
courage to stand up to them.

MARY. *(Disappointed)* Oh—gosh!

MAGGIE. It's all *Papa's* fault. He *sneaked* over to the
Penroses last night and ordered Mr. Penrose to keep
Ralph away from me!

MARY. Oh, how could he?

MAGGIE. And that's not all! The Penroses came over
on the Mayflower so Papa deliberately boasted that *he*
came over on a cattle boat!

MARY. Papa did that!

MAGGIE. Oooh—I could just— I swear I'll never speak
to Papa again.

MARY. Let's all put Papa on official silence!

(Sound of "Brennan on the Moor" upstairs.)

MAGGIE. I know what I'm going to do!

(The GIRLS *huddle around her.* MAGGIE *whispers plans
   to them. From the huddle comes an occasional
   "Right." Then the* GIRLS *slide into their places as*
   PATRICK *comes downstairs.* MAGGIE *is at the desk,
   writing a letter.* MARY *is on window seat, reading a
   magazine.* RITA *and* ROSALIE *play with their dolls at
   the Center table.)*

PATRICK. *(Entering)* Ah—I see peace has been declared at last. Good morning! *(No answer)* I said "Good morning." *(Still no answer)* Perhaps you don't quite realize who is speaking to you.

(FINNEGAN *enters from kitchen.*)

Allow me to introduce myself. I'm your father— *(Pause —then hotter)* The head of this house! And I've had just about enough of this nonsense!

FINNEGAN. What's going on now?

PATRICK. *(Crosses Left)* Now they're not speaking to me, Finnegan.

FINNEGAN. Oh—ho!

PATRICK. You know what they're up to, don't you?

FINNEGAN. *(Sits chaise)* No good.

PATRICK. They are deliberately trying to goad me into playing the tyrant. They know I detest the role so they're going to give me my fill of it. Aren't you, girls?

FINNEGAN. Ah, the subtlety of the species—even in youth. How does a mere man counter all this?

PATRICK. *(Not quite sure)* Hum—? Well—why, you keep your head, Finnegan, you keep your head. You're supposed to become angry—you remain calm. *(To the* GIRLS—*crosses above table)* Pity we can't establish communications here. I was planning to bring some things home for various people— *(No response)* Nothing much of course—some books—toys—ah well—

ROSALIE. *(With great dignity to* RITA) Would you please pass me a diaper, Rita?

RITA. *(Same dignity)* Certainly, Rosalie. *(She hands* ROSALIE *a doll diaper.)*

PATRICK. *(Above chair)* You know, Finnegan—interesting case in point here. There's a feeling that I have betrayed the democratic principles on which this family is founded—that I have therefore become a tyrant, a despot. Actually, however, there is ample precedent for my actions. I have done no more than Lincoln did during the —*Civil* War— *(He directs this at* MAGGIE's *back)* Lincoln found it necessary to—to suspend most of our democratic privileges in order to preserve the national union. And I have been forced to do the same thing in

order to preserve the unity of this family. Interesting
parallel, isn't it?

FINNEGAN. He did get shot as I recall.

PATRICK. That's irrelevant to the point. *(Sits in Morris
chair—rises as balloon pops.)*

FINNEGAN. *(Rises)* Well, President Lincoln, I leave
the matter of the reconstruction entirely in your hands.
(FINNEGAN *exits into alcove.)*

(RITA *and* ROSALIE *cross—sit chaise.)*

PATRICK. *(Sits)* Now who put that balloon under my
chair? *(Rises—crosses above chair. There is no answer)*
Now see here. I'll be answered no longer by the silence
of the morgue. When I want to live in a morgue I'll move
there. But while I'm at home with the living, we'll all
make use of the communication system God gave us! Is
that understood!

MARY. Papa doesn't know he's on official silence.

PATRICK. Well, consider it officially cancelled then!
(Pause. He regrets his outburst. Crosses Left to ROSA-
LIE*)* Ahem. I didn't mean that to sound as dictatorial as
it did, but the constitution clearly states that nobody can
be put on silence without the council's decision, so speak
up.

(ROSALIE'S *doll squeaks.)*
I said speak up!

MARY. *(Rises)* Very well, Papa. Since you order us.

PATRICK. *(Crosses below to down Right Center) I
didn't order you! (Remembering he should be more com-
posed)* I didn't order you, Mary. I simply pointed out that
you're being illegal according to the rules of our—

MARY. *(Steps in)* There aren't any rules anymore,
Papa.

PATRICK. What!

MARY. Maggie says the council is dead.

ROSALIE. She says we're living in anarchy now.

RITA. The beds aren't made either!

PATRICK. Maggie! Since when have you the right to

suspend the council! The council functions as long as I say it does!

MARY. How can you talk to her like that, Papa. After the way you've ruined her life.

PATRICK. *(Crosses Center)* Now what is this nonsense? I've ruined her life! Because I ordered that callow youth out of the house? I've preserved and extended her life!

MARY. *(Indignant, indicating quiet* MAGGIE) Just look at her, Papa. Does she look preserved and extended?

PATRICK. *(Steps Right)* Now see here, Maggie! This behavior is out of all proportion to the magnitude of events! You're trying to make a big tragic mountain out of that—that young mole hill. I'm sick of it! And I'm sick of you trying to undermine this family! Is that understood! Well, is it?

MARY. She can't answer you, Papa.

ROSALIE. Maggie has sworn an oath *never* to speak to you again.

PATRICK. *(Center)* What—?

MARY. You broke Maggie's heart, Papa. *Sneaking* over to call on Mr. Penrose like that!

PATRICK. *(Is knocked off guard by this)* What—Mr. Penrose? I—I dropped in on old Penrose to discuss the gas situation—you know my interest in that.

MARY. That wasn't all you discussed!

PATRICK. *(Still floundering)* No? Well, I—I may have mentioned something about Maggie and the boy while I was there— It's natural it would come up. But— *(Double take—steps Right)* Wait a minute! How do you know I went there?

MARY. Ralph told Maggie on the telephone. They were going to elope but you ruined everything. Now they may never even see each other again.

PATRICK. Oh, really? *(Trying to conceal his pleasure. Sits Morris chair)* The—the young man's running out on her, eh? Won't stand up to his family. Well, I thought he wouldn't.

MARY. *(Right of chair)* How could you do such a thing, Papa? Don't you love Maggie at all?

PATRICK. Now wait— *(To* MAGGIE) Ah, Maggie! I know how you feel, child. But a few months in your exciting new life at Vassar and you'll forget he ever existed.

MAGGIE. You may tell Papa I'm not going to college.

PATRICK. What—

MARY. Neither am I.

ROSALIE. Neither am I.

RITA. I'm not going neither.

ROSALIE. Either!

RITA. Either!

PATRICK. *(Rises—crosses Left)* What! Now wait a minute. You'll go to college if I have to— *(He realizes he has a few years to argue with* RITA *and* ROSALIE) In your case, forget it, I'll talk to you later! *(Crosses back to* MAGGIE *and* MARY) But *you,* Maggie, and *you*—

MAGGIE. *(Rises)* This is a letter of resignation which I have just written to Vassar. Would you be good enough to mail it for me, Mary?

PATRICK. *(Grabbing the letter)* Give me that!

MAGGIE. Tell Papa he can tear up the letter if he likes. I'll just write another and another until finally one gets out.

MARY. *(Left of chair)* She says—

PATRICK. I hear her! Maggie, please—at least give yourself time to consider.

MAGGIE. My mind is made up.

MARY. She says—

PATRICK. You tell her— Will you stop this round robin here! *(To* MAGGIE) Maggie, look, you're doing this to spite me! You're all mixed up!

MAGGIE. *(Rises)* No, Papa. I've never been more clear in my life.

PATRICK. But—the boy is out of the way—you said so yourself.

MAGGIE. *(Steps in)* Boy or no boy—the time has come for me to be independent.

PATRICK. Independent!

MAGGIE. I'm going to write a letter to Aunt Ruth. She said once she could get me a job.

PATRICK. Maggie, you'll not run out on me to do anything silly like that! You're still my daughter—a child!

MAGGIE. I'm *not* a child—I'm a woman.

(PATRICK *stares at her.*)
And I'm not going to mould my life to please you, Papa. You'd better start to realize that. You want us to fulfill your dreams—not ours. You think we're just children— to do with as you please.

PATRICK. I just want you all to grow up to be educated.

MAGGIE. You don't want us to grow up at all—any of us. I wonder how much you really love us! (*Looks at him a moment, then with a little sob she runs off upstairs.*)

MARY. (*Crosses in behind* MAGGIE *and exits—starting to cry herself*) You see, Papa. Maggie thinks you don't really love us.

ROSALIE. (*Also starting to cry—crosses to Left of* PAT- RICK *and exits upstairs*) Don't you really love us, Papa—?

RITA. (*Crosses to Left of* ROSALIE *and exits*) Papa doesn't really love us!

PATRICK. (*At foot of stairs*) *Now stop this! I do so love you! All of you, you hear!* (*Sits in Morris chair, a beaten man.*)

FINNEGAN. (*Who has come out for the disturbance*) An incredible species. (*Gives* PATRICK *a drink.*)

(PATRICK *sits in his chair muttering to himself. At this point* MRS. GALLUP *enters front door.*)

MRS. GALLUP. Hello, Mr. Finnegan. (*Seeing* PATRICK) Is everything all right? (*Crosses to* FINNEGAN, *Left Center.*)

FINNEGAN. We're all a little bit bewildered at the moment, mam.

(PATRICK *rises, crosses to sit in window.*)
And did you have a satisfactory session at the bank?

MRS. GALLUP. Oh, yes, Mr. Finnegan. I have the money right here. (*She shows it to him.*)

FINNEGAN. *(Starts to reach for it)* You may not know it, mam, but I'll be indebted to you for the rest of my life.

MRS. GALLUP. I—I—dropped in to see Madame Jeremiah on the way back—

FINNEGAN. How are all the spirits doing? I assume we have their full blessing regarding this—little matter—

MRS. GALLUP. Oh—yes. I have Madame Jeremiah's message right here. I guess it's all right for me to read it to you— *(Takes out message)*

>"As wife to be
>Dispense free-ly
>As widow still
>Give nothing till."

(She snaps her purse with a finality that makes FINNE-GAN'S *face fall, and exits into the kitchen.* FINNEGAN *sits in Morris chair.* PATRICK *hands him a drink, then sits in arm chair Left.)*

PATRICK. That's all I ever asked of them. First college —then marriage.

FINNEGAN. *(Regarding kitchen)* Marriage is out of the question.

PATRICK. Not after college. I don't expect them to remain spinsters.

FINNEGAN. If only Adam had had the sense to keep his ribs to himself!

PATRICK. *(Rises—crosses up)* I don't understand them. Maggie says I don't want them to grow up. Ye Gods, if they only would! Ah, Finnegan, you can thank the Lord you have no women in your family.

FINNEGAN. I mention the fact in my prayers daily.

PATRICK. *(Above chair)* Women can be so unreasonable.

FINNEGAN. Your female mind is not constructed—how shall I say—well—it's just not constructed.

PATRICK. Men are not unreasonable like women.

FINNEGAN. Take my case for example. Would a *man* ever hound me for alimony?

PATRICK. Well, I—I'll have to think about your problem some other time, Finnegan. Right now I'm just about on the ropes. *(Sits chair.)*

FINNEGAN. *(Rises)* Ah—I wish I could help you with *your* problem, Patrick. But just the thought of four girls immobilizes my judgment. Have you ever considered simply—giving up?

PATRICK. What do you mean giving up? You mean— let her get married?

FINNEGAN. It's a horrible thought I know. But at least it's a chance for peace.

PATRICK. Yes, but at what a price. Now if she wanted to marry a *man*—maybe. But that boy! That spineless— memo-writing vice president—afraid of his parents— afraid of me—

(Sound of CAR.)

What's that?

FINNEGAN. I think it's the Vice President.

PATRICK. *(Rises—crosses to door)* Why the gall of the creature—sneaking back here!

(RITA and ROSALIE appear on stairs.)

Now you stay out of this! *(Crosses to RITA and ROSALIE.)*

(The GIRLS go upstairs.)

You know what he thinks, don't you? He thinks I'm away at work.

FINNEGAN. You going to let him in?

PATRICK. How can I throw him out if I don't let him in?

RALPH. *(Entering)* Mr. Flannigan, I'm certainly glad to find you home.

PATRICK. You are—?

RALPH. Sir, you made a great impression on me yesterday.

PATRICK. I did?

FINNEGAN. Well!

RALPH. Good morning, Mr. Finnegan. *(Crosses down Right.)*

(PATRICK crosses Left of RALPH.)

You were right, sir. I had no business down there in my

family's company. So I took action. As of this morning I am out of gas!

PATRICK. What!

RALPH. Furthermore, you may be interested to know, I am going into electricity.

PATRICK. Are you now?

RALPH. I was wasting my time down there and I thank you for pointing it out, sir. *(He pumps* PATRICK's *surprised hand gratefully. Crosses Left)* Now, sir, there's something else we have to discuss. About Maggie, sir. I'm sorry to say this but if you don't consent to our marriage I'm going to elope with her!

PATRICK. I think as her father I'll have something to say about that!

RALPH. *(To* PATRICK) Mr. Flannigan! Fatherhood may be a great institution but by George, sir, you carry it too far!

PATRICK. Is that so—?

RALPH. You treat her like a child. But she isn't a child, she's a grownup.

PATRICK. Well, maybe she is grownup, my boy, but—

RALPH. And don't call me a boy! I'm just as much of a man as your daughter—

FINNEGAN. I think we might even say more so, don't you?

RALPH. *(Crosses up Left to* FINNEGAN) Now, Mr. Finnegan, you keep out of this—sir! *(To* PATRICK) Well, Mr. Flannigan, are you going to be reasonable?

PATRICK. *(Crosses up)* Young man, I am not accustomed to being addressed like this—

RALPH. Violence is no solution but I'm warning you, sir—

FINNEGAN. *(Between them)* All right, all right. Nobody's going to fight here, are we, Patrick?

PATRICK. I'm not so sure.

(ROSALIE *enters at top of stairs, listens.*)

FINNEGAN. Now, this young man has come here with

a very different attitude, don't you think so, Patrick.

PATRICK. Well—maybe you're right. Sit down, young man. I think we'd like to ask you some questions.

(ROSALIE *exits.*)

RALPH. Does that mean, sir, that you are ready to reconsider?

PATRICK. We are going to ask you the questions. Sit down.

RALPH. All right. *(He sits Left of table.)*

(FINNEGAN *above table.*)

PATRICK. Now you say you're in electricity?

(RITA *enters at top of stairs, listens.*)

RALPH. Yes, sir. And I'm starting at the bottom. Ten dollars a week.

PATRICK. Well—well—what did your parents say to all this?

RALPH. Well, sir, as a matter of fact, as of this morning we're not on speaking terms.

PATRICK. *(Crosses down and Left to sit chaise)* That seems to be contagious today. So you stood up to your family, eh?

RALPH. Yes, sir. And when I told them I was going to marry Maggie, they disinherited me.

(RITA *exits.*)

PATRICK. Oh!

FINNEGAN. *(Rises)* So you're broke. Why the gall of this man. He barges in here and proposes marriage on ten dollars a week. I suppose you plan to come here and sponge off the bounty of Mr. Flannigan!

RALPH. Sir, I had no such thing in my mind. No, sir!

Grandfather Penrose left me all the money I'll ever need —and to spare.

FINNEGAN. And to spare— *(Double take)* And to spare? *(Sits Morris chair.)*

RALPH. Yes, sir! I suppose you could say I'm independently wealthy.

FINNEGAN. *(His self-interest aroused)* Could you now? Ah, Patrick, in light of what this young man has been telling us, I think we should reopen our minds to this whole matter of marriage.

RALPH. By George! Well, thank you, Mr. Finnegan.

PATRICK. Now, Finnegan, this is my problem—

FINNEGAN. *(Rises; crosses to him)* Patrick, I know you well. You're stubborn as a mule. But this is one time when I think you've got to admit you're wrong—

PATRICK. What's gotten into you, Finnegan?

FINNEGAN. Well, to be honest—this young man's sterling qualities have quite overcome me. And I'd hate to see us lose him. *(Crosses Right above.)*

PATRICK. Now just a minute—I'll make up my mind about this boy in my own good time—

FINNEGAN. You're a stubborn man, Patrick.

PATRICK. I'll not be pushed.

(ROSALIE *re-enters.)*

FINNEGAN. Won't you now? Well, then I find myself on the side of the girls. And I tell you this. If I sat in your family council right now, for your own good, I'd vote for the marriage. And do you know something else? By the Lord Harry, I think you'd vote for it too. *(He absentmindedly bangs the table with a glass for emphasis.)*

ROSALIE. Are you calling a meeting of the family council, Mr. Finnegan?

FINNEGAN. No, I was— *(He gets an idea)* Yes! I hereby call a meeting of the family council.

PATRICK. What! *(Rises.)*

ROSALIE. *(Calling off up stairs)* Maggie—Rita—Mary—

FINNEGAN. Yes, Patrick, you yourself gave me the right. And what's more this is one time you'll not be able to sway the votes of us little ones.

(The GIRLS *all come down except* MAGGIE.)

And it's my turn to be Madam Chairman! Ladies, take your usual places.

(They sit.)

(To the hesitating MAGGIE *up stairs, still invisible)* Will *all* the ladies please take their usual places.

(MAGGIE *appears.* RALPH *leads* MAGGIE *down.)*

Ladies and gentlemen, I have called this special session of the Flannigan family council in order that we may hear from a man who is not unfamiliar to you—your father. Patrick, you went back on this council yesterday —and the council was laid to rest because of it. Now admit this—you've missed it. And so have I for that matter. It's a far better system than we've had since. Patrick, won't you join the council again?

MARY. Please, Papa.

ROSALIE. Won't you please, Papa?

RITA. Please, Papa.

MAGGIE. You have missed it, Papa? We have—

PATRICK. I am to say the least—overwhelmed. *(Pause. Rises)* Maggie—and all of you. The battle's been long and instructive. There have been casualties on both sides. I have in no way changed my views on the importance of college. However, I know now I can't rub your noses in education. You must want it for yourselves. You fought a good fight and I shall abide by the council's decision of yesterday. So Maggie—I surrender my sword to you. And to you, Mary—and Rosalie—and Rita. Maggie—do you really want to marry this boy? *(Above* MAGGIE.)

MAGGIE. Yes, I do, Papa.

PATRICK. Very well.

FINNEGAN. Meeting adjourned.

MAGGIE. *(Rises, embraces* RALPH *and* PATRICK) Oh, Papa, you darling. Could Ralph stay to dinner?

PATRICK. Of course. When I surrender I surrender on all fronts. He'll be welcome to dinner. I'll go further, son. You're welcome into this family. *(He offers* RALPH *his hand.)*

RALPH. *(Takes it)* Thank you, sir. It's sure some family to be in. Would it be all right if Maggie and I—go for a spin, sir?

PATRICK. All right, all right—

ROSALIE. Can we go too, Papa.

MARY. I want to go too.

PATRICK. Go on—go on—take them all with you.

RALPH. But—

ROSALIE. Come on, Rita. We'll ride in the front.

(They run out front d

MAGGIE. Ralph, start the car. I want to talk to Papa alone for a minute.

FINNEGAN. Come along, boy. I'll help you crank it.

RALPH. I tell you, Mr. Finnegan, I'm so grateful to you, sir. I—I don't know how I can *ever* repay you—

*(*FINNEGAN *knows how he can. He puts his arm on* RALPH's *shoulder and exits with his catch.)*

MAGGIE. Oh, Papa—you're such a dear. I—I made things difficult for you, didn't I?

PATRICK. You're a stubborn girl—a piece of myself.

MAGGIE. You do understand—don't you. It had to be this way—

PATRICK. I know. I know. I didn't realize—you'd become a woman! It's all gone so fast, hasn't it— Mrs. Ralph Penrose! *(He puts a finger under her chin—kisses her)* Well—run along now—

FINNEGAN. *(In doorway. Calling off)* All best wishes, Maggie.

*(*MAGGIE *exits.)*

PATRICK. Finnegan, I think we could use a drink.

FINNEGAN. Oddly enough, I can always use one.

PATRICK. Well, there goes Maggie. It's like letting the heart's blood go.

FINNEGAN. Maybe it was wrong of me— Pushing you to a decision like that.

PATRICK. Hum? No—you did the right thing.

FINNEGAN. *(Thoughtfully eyeing cubicle and then looking upstairs)* Well, at least there'll be a guest room now.

PATRICK. *(Chuckling)* Oh, Finnegan, you're incorrigible! *(Warmly)* Well, I'll be needing you around here more than ever now that Maggie is gone—

FINNEGAN. Patrick! You have lost a daughter and gained a son!

(MARY *enters with callow youth.)*

MARY. Papa, this is Richard O'Connor. He lives next door—

RICHARD. Mr. Flannigan, sir—

PATRICK. *(The last straw) No!*

CURTAIN

THE LOUD RED PATRICK

SOUND EQUIPMENT

Tape recorder—double amplifier
3 speakers and cables
1 intercom
2 monitors
4 speakers and cables

Cue 1 Car arriving—then idling—then leaving
Cue 2 Hurdy-gurdy
Cue 3 Car arriving
Cue 4 Car leaving
Cue 5 Car arriving
Cue 6 Sousa band
Cue 7 Car arriving
Cue 8 Hurdy-gurdy

THE LOUD RED PATRICK

PROP LIST

Furniture
Morris chair
Footstool
Oval table
Round table
Armchair
3 straight back chairs
Chaise lounge
Secretary
Victrola (circa 1912)
Hat rack
Sideboard
Occasional chair
Pedestal
Waste basket

Flowers and Shrubs
Assorted small roses
3 potted ferns
Assorted flowers in nosegay
Assorted shrubs and vines for porch and windows
Hanging pot of ivy

Toys
Large panda
2 small stuffed animals
Pop-gun
Balloons (sausage type)
Pea-shooter
Large mama doll

Small rag doll
"Holgate" blockmixer
Large ambulance
2 red cross headbands

Pictures
4 large oval pictures
3 large square pictures
Large painting of young woman
2 small square pictures
2 small oval pictures

Carpet
Set—all playing area including runner for stairs

Miscellaneous Props
Cap
Raincoat
Cane
Jacket
Record
Two small ashtrays w/matchboxes
Small antique clock
Large antique standing clock
Antique alarm clock
Antique jewel box
Antique inkwell
Covered pad
Straight nib pen
2 china figureens
2 glass wine decanters
Bowl of waxed fruit w/"live" apples
Mersham pipe
Cigar humidor
Tobacco humidor
6 wine glasses
2 tumblers
Whiskey bottle w/cork
Large ashtray w/matchbox
Square tray

Round tray
Assorted books
New book
Stethoscope
Briefcase
Box of packages
2 cups and saucers
Beer mug
4 neckties on string
Comforter
Small vase
Sewing basket
Trick straw hat
Gavel
2 5 x 8 pads of plain paper
2 pencils
Bible
Small pail w/2 cowbells attached to handle and fish line
    attached to handle w/clip for hooking Victrola
    starter
Straw broom with can tied to it
Mop
Spatula
Bottle opener
Small pads
Coins
Package paper money
Old-fashioned suitcase w/umbrella attached
Pair old-fashioned glasses
Powdered rosin
Two prop newspapers
Prop magazine
2 prop letters
Glass crash
Pine crash
Door slam
Sunbonnet
4 cushions

2 built-in seat covers
2 andirons
Fire fence
Fire poker and shovel
Paper fan
Pipe rack w/3 pipes
Candle snuffer
2 plaster busts
Doll diapers
Bulb horn
Hand door bell
Can of tobacco
Cigars
Bottles of stout
.22 blanks
.22 blank pistol
Oval tablecloth w/ball fringe

Set items as follows for all three acts

Hatrack
Cap, raincoat, cane, jacket, sunbonnet

Sideboard
Large standing clock (shelf type), 2 figureens, 2 potted
   ferns, decanter of wine, square tray w/decanter of
   wine and 6 wine glasses, 2 tumblers, large ashtray
   w/matchbox

Oval table
Small ashtrays w/matchboxes, pipe

Round Table
Sewing basket—books/under

Secretary
Small standing clock (shelf type), inkwells, straight pen,
   covered pad, 2 pads and pencils, bank, gavel, writing
   paper and envelopes

Pedestal
Pot of ferns

There are lace curtains over all windows and drapes by
    bay window
Sliding drapes cover alcove (see ground plan)
Front door bell hangs next to front door
Book on bay window seat

Wall Decorations as follows (refer to ground plan)
2 large oval pictures
Hanging pot of ivy
Large square picture, 2 small square pictures
Large square picture, 2 large oval pictures, 1 bust, 1
    candle snuffer
Bust, 2 small oval pictures
Pipe rack w/3 pipes, 2 small plates
Large painting of young woman, 2 large plates
Large square picture
Paper fan in light over door
Wall telephone

For furniture placement see ground plan

Preset Act One

Oval Table
Fruit bowl, cigar humidor, tobacco humidor

Sideboard
Whiskey bottle, full, cork alongside to Right and behind
    2 tumblers

Prop Table Stage Right
Suitcase w/umbrella, straw hat, nosegay, rosin, box of
    packages, prop letter, small pad, coins, briefcase
    w/new book, stethoscope, prop newspaper, Patrick's
    hat

Prop Table Stage Left
2 cups and soucers, round tray, bottle of stout, prop
    coffee, bottle opener, spatula, beer mug

Head of Stairs
Pea-shooter, mama doll, doll diapers, inflated balloons, pop-gun, 2 stuffed animals, pail w/cowbells and string, Bible, rag doll

Morris Chair
Broken balloon behind chair in slats
Footstool tied to front of Morris chair

Close drapes on alcove ¾—these are sliding drapes

Alcove
Blockmixer and ambulance on seat, large panda sits on floor in front of seat

Q1 Blow bulb horn offstage Right
Q2 Doorslam

Preset Act Two
Oval Table
5 x 8 pad and pencil
Strike fruit bowl, cigar humidor, tobacco humidor

Sideboard
Whiskey bottle full, cork in, set on lower Left hand corner

Round Table
Set small vase assorted roses

Alcove
Set comforter on bench
Strike blockmixer and panda
Set footstool midway between Morris chair and curtain line

Chaise Lounge
Set ambulance in upper Right hand corner
Set briefcase on sweep seat under cushion proper—leave head of stairs alone

Lower window half way

Strike all else from set

Q1 Pick up box of packages
Q2 Doorslam
Q3 Bulb horn

Preset Act Three

Oval Table
Set cigar humidor
Strike pad and pencil

Head of Stairs
Set can w/cowbells out and string free
Strike new book, stethoscope, red cross headbands

Round Table
Strike small vase of roses
Strike coins from bank to prop table
Place gavel in convenient place for curtain calls
Set pipe and glass crashes

Pour prop coffee and open stout bottle
Set footstool stage Right and next to Morris chair
Set broom and mop against front door buck
Set stage Left straight chair next to oval table

Q1 Glass rattle
Q2 Pipe crash
Q3 Glass crash
Q4 Pick up clock (alarm)
Q5 Pick up broom and mop
Q6 Door slam
Q7 Door slam
Q8 Glass crash
Q9 Pick up tray w/cups and saucers
Q10 Fire .22 blank pistol

THE LOUD RED PATRICK

COSTUME PLOT

PATRICK

Act One

Brown suit, blue and white striped shirt, white collar, red tie, black shoes, red socks, green suspenders, brown derby hat.

Act Two

First entrance: Salt and pepper brown tweed trousers, blue and white striped shirt with white collar, red tie, black shoes, red socks, black and red suspenders

Second entrance: Same as above, plus coat to tweed suit

Act Three

First entarnce: Same as Act Two—minus collar and tie and jacket—plus blue apron

Second entrance: Same as Act Two—second entrance

FINNEGAN

Act One

Black and white checked suit, white shirt, beige vest, blue and white polka-dotted bow tie, black shoes, red and black striped socks, white spats, yellow gloves, green arm suspenders, gray derby hat, pocket handkerchief, green suspenders

Act Two

First entrance: Same as Act One except red and gray striped bow tie

Second entrance: Same except no hat, gloves, coat

Third entrance: Tie askew

Act Three

First entrance: White shirt with blue and white striped dickey front, no collar, no tie, no shoes, no spats, red arm suspenders

Rest of Act: Shoes on

MRS. GALLUP

Act One

First entrance: Brown skirt, green and white checked blouse, white lace collar with brown bow, black shoes, tan hose, gold-rimmed glasses, blue apron

Second entrance: Same, except no apron

Act Two

First entrance: Same as Act Two—plus jacket to match skirt and black straw hat with pheasant feathers

Second entrance: Same as Act One—second entrance

Act Three

Lavender and white patterned dress, same shoes, white hose, black and white feather boa, same hat, black purse

MARY

Act One

Green plaid jumper dress, white blouse, black shoes, black hose, red hair ribbon, red cardigan sweater

Act Two

Yellow party dress, white shoes, white hose, yellow hair ribbon

Act Three

Same as Act Two except no sweater

MAGGIE

Act One

White blouse, green skirt, green jacket, black shoes, black hose, straw hat with patterned tie ribbon, black hair ribbon

Act Two

First entrance: White party dress, white shoes, white hose, pink hair ribbon

Second entrance: Same plus light green sash with a pink rose thereon

Act Three

Same as Act One except no hat, no jacket

RALPH

Act Two

Blue jacket, white shirt, cream trousers, blue and white polka dot bow tie, white buck shoes, black socks, yellow plaid vest, pink boutonniere, white handkerchief, straw hat

Act Three

Brown suit, white shirt, maroon tie, brown vest, brown shoes, black socks, tan duster, tan cap with goggles

ROSALIE

Act One

First entrance: White middie blouse with red trimming, red skirt, black shoes, black stockings, black hair ribbon, green cape

Second entrance: Same minus cape, plus red cross head band

Third entrance: Same, minus head band

Act Two

Blue dress, white stockings, black shoes, blue hair ribbon

Act Three

Same as Act One, third entrance

RITA

Act One

First entrance: White middie blouse with blue trimming,

navy blue skirt, black shoes, black stockings, red
hair ribbons, red cape

Second entrance: Same minus cape, plus red cross head
band

Third entrance: Same, minus head band

Act Two

Pink dress, white stockings, black shoes, pink hair ribbon

Act Three

Same as Act One, third entrance

RICHARD

Act Three

White shirt, no tie, red and yellow striped blazer, brown
and beige striped trousers, beige shoes, brown socks

ELECTRICAL EQUIPMENT AND ITS USE

SWITCHBOARDS

BOARD ONE

Location	Instrument	Plug Boxes	Plate and No.
Balcony	6-6" Leko	1-6 wax	3000- 1
Balcony	6-6" Leko	1-6 wax	3000- 2
Balcony	6-6" Leko	1-6 wax	3000- 3
1st Pipe	6-6" Fresnels	1-4 wax	3000- 4
1st Pipe	2 sections	1-4 wax	3000- 5
1st Pipe	300 watt par border	1-4 wax	3000- 6
1st Pipe	Circuits 1-2-3	1-4 wax	3000- 7
2nd Pipe	6-6" Fresnels	1-4 wax	3000- 8
2nd Pipe	6-6" Fresnels	1-4 wax	3000- 9
2nd Pipe	6-6" Fresnels	1-4 wax	3000-10
Boom Left	6-6" Leko	1-4 wax	3000-11
Boom Right	6-6" Leko	1-4 wax	3000-12

97

BOARD TWO

Location	Instrument	Plug Boxes	Plate and No.
Boom Right	3-8" 1000 watt Fresnels	1-4 wax	3000-13
Boom U.C.	2-8" 1000 watt Fresnels	1-4 wax	3000-14
	1-6" 500 watt Fresnels		
	4-6" 500 watt Fresnels		
Boom U.L.C.	1 wiz 250 watt Fresnels	1-4 wax	3000-15
Aux. S.B.			3000-16
Aux. S.B.			3000-17
Cy. X-Ray	2 sections } 300 watt par border circuits 1-2-3	1-4 wax	3000-18
Cy. X-Ray		1-4 wax	3000-19
Cy. X-Ray		1-4 wax	3000-20
Floor Cy. X-Ray	1 section } 300 watt par border circuits 1-2-3	1-4 wax	3000-21
		1-4 wax	3000-22
		1-4 wax	3000-23

AUX. BOARD

Location	Instrument	Plate and No.
2nd pipe	Fresnel 23—2 way jumper to bracket 1	500— 1
2nd pipe	Fresnel 17—2 way jumper to bracket 2	500— 2
2nd pipe	Fresnel 3—2 way jumper to bracket 3	500— 3
2nd pipe	Fresnel 10—2 way jumper to bracket 4	500— 4

Location	Instrument	Plate No.
2nd pipe	Fresnel 8—special	5
2nd pipe	Fresnel 13—special	6
Kitchen door L.	Wizard 250 watt	7
Stair	1-6" Leko on boom	8
Stair	1-6" Fresnel on boom	

BLANK

FOCUS AND COLOR CHART

Location	Instrument	Brig. Color	Focus
Balcony L. to R.	1—6" Leko	2	L.—door
Balcony L. to R.	2—6" Leko	51	L.—end of couch
Balcony L. to R.	3—6" Leko	17	L.—couch
Balcony L. to R.	4—6" Leko	2	L.—head of couch
Balcony L. to R.	5—6" Leko	W	L.—Center
Balcony L. to R.	6—6" Leko	51	L.—end C. table
Balcony L. to R.	7—6" Leko	17	C.—table
Balcony L. to R.	8—6" Leko	17	L.—head of couch
Balcony L. to R.	9—6" Leko	2	L.—Center
Balcony L. to R.	10—6" Leko	17	L.—head of couch

500—9
500—10
500—11
500—12

Location	Instrument	Brig. Color	Focus
Balcony L. to R.	11—6" Leko	51	R.—C. table
Balcony L. to R.	12—6" Leko	2	R.—chair of C. table
Balcony L. to R.	13—6" Leko	W	R. of C. table
Balcony L. to R.	14—6" Leko	2	R.—C.
Balcony L. to R.	15—6" Leko	2	R.—chair of C. table
Balcony L. to R.	16—6" Leko	W	R.—table R.
Balcony L. to R.	17—6" Leko	17	R.—desk R.
Balcony L. to R.	18—6" Leko	2	R.—desk R.

In Three Circuits

1—1-4-7-10-13-16
2—2-5-8-11-14-17
3—3-6-9-12-15-18

	Instrument	Brig. Color	Focus
1st pipe	6-6" Fresnels	62	
1st pipe	2 sections	62	
1st pipe	300 watt par border	2	Gen. lighting
1st pipe	circuits 1-2-3	17	

{ 300 watt par border, circuits 1-2-3 braced together }

Location	Instrument	Color	Focus
2nd pipe	23-6" Fresnels 1-6" Leko set up in 3 groups of 6 each and 6 specials		
Cir.—1	1- 5; 14-19; 20-22	17	L. to R. sweep

Location	Instrument	Color	Focus
Cir.—2	2- 6; 4- 7; 16-21	62	C. to R. sweep
Cir.—3	9-11; 12-15; 18-24	2	C. to L. sweep
Specials	Fresnel 3-2 way jumper to bracket 1	62	Bracket 1
	Fresnel 10-2 way jumper to bracket 2	62	Bracket 2
	Fresnel 17-2 way jumper to bracket 3	62	Bracket 3
	Fresnel 23-2 way jumper to bracket 4	62	Bracket 4
	Fresnel 8	2	Telephone U.C.
Boom L.	Fresnel 13	62	on C. door
Boom U.C.	12' pipe 3-8" 1000 watt Fresnels	62	window R.
Boom U.C.	12' pipe 2-8" 1000 watt Fresnels	62	Back of window U.C.
Cy. X-Ray	1-6" 500 watt Fresnels	62	porch
Boom U.C.	12' pipe 3-6" 500 watt Fresnels	62	Door C.
Floor X-Ray	2 sec. 300 watt par border cir. 1	62	Back of windows
	2 sec. 300 watt par border cir. 2	W	L. and C.
	2 sec. 300 watt par border cir. 3	17	
	1 sec. 300 watt par border cir. 1	17	
	1 sec. 300 watt par border cir. 2	17	
Kitchen door L.	1 sec. 300 watt par border cir. 3	17	
	Wizard 250 watt	62	

Instrument

4 gas brackets—glass shades—practical
1 chandelier—glass shades—prop
1 hanging lamp—hallway—prop
1 bell for clock alarm
1 candle taper

THE LOUD RED PATRICK

LIGHT CUES

ACT ONE

Preset $\dfrac{4\text{-}5\text{-}6\text{-}7\text{-}8\text{-}9\text{-}11\text{-}12}{F}$

$\dfrac{13\text{-}14\text{-}15}{2\frac{1}{2}}$ $\dfrac{16\text{-}17\text{-}18\text{-}19\text{-}20}{F}$ $\dfrac{21\text{-}22\text{-}23}{3}$

Aux. $\dfrac{8\text{-}9\text{-}10}{2}$ $\dfrac{11\text{-}12}{F}$

Cue 1—$\dfrac{1\text{-}2\text{-}3}{F}$

Cue 2—$\dfrac{21\text{-}22\text{-}23}{7}$ $\dfrac{20}{5}$ $\dfrac{13\text{-}14\text{-}15}{4}$

$\dfrac{11\text{-}12}{5}$ $\dfrac{1}{3}$ $\dfrac{2\text{-}3}{3}$

Cue 3—Aux 1 to F

Cue 4—Aux 2 to F

Cue 5—Aux 3 to F

Cue 6—Aux 4 to F

Then 1-2-3 to F

Act Rail D. & O.

ACT TWO

Preset $\dfrac{4\text{-}5\text{-}6\text{-}7\text{-}8\text{-}9\text{-}11\text{-}12}{F}$

$\dfrac{13\text{-}14\text{-}15}{2}$ $\dfrac{17\text{-}18\text{-}19\text{-}20}{F}$ $\dfrac{21\text{-}22\text{-}23}{3}$

Aux $\dfrac{8\text{-}9\text{-}10}{2}$ $\dfrac{11\text{-}12}{F}$

Cue 7 — $\dfrac{1\text{-}2\text{-}3}{F}$

Act Rail D. & O.

ACT THREE

Preset $\dfrac{4\text{-}5\text{-}6\text{-}7\text{-}8\text{-}9\text{-}10\text{-}11\text{-}12}{F}$

$\dfrac{13\text{-}14\text{-}15}{F}$ $\dfrac{17\text{-}18\text{-}19\text{-}20}{F}$ $\dfrac{21\text{-}22\text{-}23}{3}$

Aux $\dfrac{8\text{-}9\text{-}10}{2}$ $\dfrac{11\text{-}12}{F}$

Cue 8 — $\dfrac{1\text{-}2\text{-}3}{F}$